MW00676187

Athlete's Way of Excellence

ToBE

PHOTO CREDIT: © KIRBY LEE- USA TODAY SPORTS

"In the book The Athletes Way of Excellence, Tobe highlights concepts that I have used not only in sports, but also in my life. I have been privileged to know Tobe since my early years at Stanford, and the philosophies that are portrayed in this book are the same ones he taught me during a few of my struggles.

The Way of Excellence is not about tangible evidence, but rather the pursuit for greatness.

He taught me that there's only one person who can judge your success and that's you as an individual. Only you know whether or not you gave your best effort to God, your family, your teammates, and yourself, or whoever you play for.

He has inspired me that you win or you learn. You never lose. There is something to learn and grow from in every situation. I'm excited to see the impact this book will have on many, as it did my own life."

-Christian McCaffrey, *Carolina Panthers formerly Stanford Cardinal*

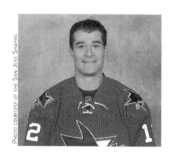

PHOTO COURTESY OF THE SAN JOSE SHARKS

"Tobe has helped me in so many ways in my career. Applying the lessons in this book will help any athlete get to the next level. Continuing to practice the lessons once you have reached the highest level in your sport will help you stay on top of your game."

-Patrick Marleau, *Toronto Maple Leafs, formerly San Jose Sharks, two time Olympic gold medalist for Canada 2010 & 2014*

"Working with Tobe has helped me reach my full potential. His insight has not only helped me perform at my best but live a healthier life away from hockey. The tools he provides in this book will help any athlete fully enjoy their sport as well as perform better both mentally and physically."

-Martin Jones, *San Jose Sharks*

"Through my work with Tobe, I learned the importance to communicate, speak up, and be assertive about my needs to my coach and choreographer. Tell them what works for me and what does not, so that I could be on a path of continuous growth. Today, I choreograph my own routines and design my own costumes."

-Karen Chen, *2017 U.S. National figure skating champion and 2018 Olympian*

Athlete's Way of Excellence

ANCIENT CHINESE WISDOM REVEALING THE
SECRETS TO MODERN DAY ATHLETIC PEAK
PERFORMANCE AND HOW TO BE IN THE ZONE

Tobe Hanson

One Source Unlimited, Inc.
Pleasanton, California

One Source Unlimited, Inc.
7090 Johnson Drive
Pleasanton, CA 94588
Phone: 1-925-400-9932
Email: 1SourceUnlimitedInc@gmail.com

For more information visit:
www.TobeHanson.com

Printed in the United States of America:
Paperback ISBN: 978-0-9990601-4-8
Hardback ISBN: 978-0-9990601-5-5
Library of Congress Control Number: 2018946426
First Edition

Author's Disclaimer

To the best of my knowledge, the principles offered in the *Athlete's Way of Excellence* are not in opposition to any religion, they are not intended to be dogmatic in nature, nor are they designed to create or support any form of cultist doctrine. I have seasoned my own conclusions and understandings of ancient Chinese philosophy, the Law of the Five Elements, and the Law of the Four Seasons with my personal interpretations of biblical scriptures and thirty-three years of practice studying human performance, as well as the cause of failure, tension, and pain. These principles can be applied by any athlete, regardless of age or athletic ability, to improve physical and mental performance as well as to increase the joy of competing and playing the game.

The cover photo is showing Christian McCaffrey #5 returning a kick for Stanford against the Washington Huskies on September 30, 2016. The Stanford logo has been removed from his helmet, jersey and pants due to Stanford's position on commercial use of its trademark. Photo by Otto Greule Jr. Licensed for commercial use by Getty Images.

In the Way of Excellence, the true purpose is to have fun competing, to be challenged and get better, to commit to mastery in your athletic endeavor, and to experience moments of excellence.

Acknowledgements

When I look up on the walls in my office and see the many pictures of athletes I worked on during the last 30 years, I am struck with gratitude.

To take part in an athlete's recovery from an agonizing sports injury, to be able to help him or her improve their performance and to pursue their dreams, to experience the glory in their victories and the agony in their defeat, has been extremely gratifying. With each picture and every athlete comes a priceless memory.

I am grateful to each and every athlete who was a patient of mine for letting me be part of their striving for excellence in their sport and athletic pursuit.

All this time, over three decades, I have strived to reach my own excellence – to develop a therapy that gives instant results in healing sports injuries, as well as find teachings that would improve performance of body and mind.

I have learned from every athlete, every injury and every experience to get a little better day by day. As much as I have learned, I still consider myself a student because I am still learning every day. In my opinion, a master is someone who knows it all; there is a difference between striving for perfection and considering yourself a master.

I am forever grateful to Ray Tuft, the head Athletic Trainer for the San Jose Sharks, for opening the door and giving me the opportunity to work with the Sharks hockey players since the late 1990s.

I also want to thank Mike Potenza, the Sharks Strength and Conditioning Coach, for our collaboration and constant search for ways to speed up recovery and improve performance of team athletes.

I want to thank the entire San Jose Sharks management and each and all the Sharks players I worked on for the amazing ride and years of excitement.

I want to thank Eitan Gelber, director of Athletic Training, and the Stanford Athletics Department for being open to new, alternative sports medicine therapies and for inviting me to aid with the recovery of their football players. I am grateful for the opportunity to get to know each and every one of the Stanford football players I have had the pleasure to work with during the 2016 and 2017 season.

I am very grateful for the opportunity to work with, and get to know, the great character of Christian McCaffrey, Patrick Marleau, Karen Chen and Martin Jones, and for their demonstration of the Way of Excellence in their sport.

I am forever grateful for the tireless work, encouragement and excitement from Peggi Speers in getting this book manifested in print and publication. I also want to thank Sheila Shaw for her design and layout of the cover of the book, as well as internal book illustrations.

I also want to thank my office manager Tracey Montoya for all her help with editing and proof reading on short notices.

I cannot in words express how grateful I am for all the help I received from my dear friend Sam Awad. Sam always took time to help and make me laugh in spite of the fact that he is the busiest person I know.

Most of all, I want to thank Sue, my loving wife and best friend, for the endless support she gave me to follow my passion. Sue has spent endless hours reading over and editing my early scripts of this book. She is always unselfishly happy and excited for me even when I am away from her to work on athletes.

This book is dedicated to my love of sports and athletics and it is my hope that it shall provide the wisdom to young and aspiring athletes that most athletes never fully learn or learn too late in their career.

East meets West

This book is a fusion of Ancient Chinese Philosophy and modern day Sports Psychology

The Zone is when you are being intensely aware of what you are doing in that instant.

Author's Notes:
How This Book Came to Be

I have been practicing my skills and developed my own form of manual therapy, a holistic form of Sports Medicine, since 1984. This therapy is a fusion of modern day sports medicine and ancient day Chinese medicine.

For more than twenty years, I have provided thousands of treatments to professional athletes. I have worked as a muscle therapy consultant for the San Jose Sharks medical team since the late 1990s and also worked with athletes from the NHL, NFL, UFC, PGA, MLB as well as Olympians in swimming, track and field and figure skating, to fix their pain, restore their function and improve their performance.

Over the years, as I continued to study and improve my skills, I got better at understanding and incorporating the ancient Chinese wisdom into my therapy. I was able to explain cause and effect as it relates to an individual's injury, health or dis-ease. From this insight came my first book, *The Four Seasons Way of Life, Ancient Wisdom for Healing and Personal Growth*.

In my love of sports and continued studies of ancient Chinese philosophy, I kept searching for a way to explain how ancient masters of Zen and kung fu perfected their skills thousands of years ago. I envisioned that this ancient way could teach modern day athletes how to perform in excellence. Today's athlete often has a tendency to over analyze, think too much, and try too hard. There is an excessive and anxious focus on the outcome or result of their athletic experience. They anxiously, fearfully over focus on the thinking and "doing" and miss the experience of "being" in the present moment. Yet, the only time an athlete can experience true peak performance is when he or she is in the Zone; a euphoric state of effortless "being" when there is no thinking, just going with the flow, responding to the circumstances and creating outside the box.

During the last few years when working with San Jose Sharks hockey players, I had started to incorporate the ancient Chinese teachings to those who were interested in looking into their own behavior and mind for healing of their injuries.

In spring 2016, I received a text from Stanford's running back, Christian McCaffrey. Christian was referred to me by Ray Tuft the athletic trainer for the San Jose Sharks. His text message said he'd been looking to find someone to help him get his body right. He said his muscles felt tight, and he felt a step slower since finishing the season.

Christian had a monster breakout sophomore season in 2015. He broke Barry Sanders's NCAA record of 3,250 all-purpose yards, finishing with 3,864. He was a consensus All-American and was the Associated Press College Football Player of the Year and Pac-12 Player of the Year. Christian finished second in the 2015 Heisman Trophy voting. During the 2016 Rose Bowl, the last game of his 2015 season, he became the first player to rush for over 100 yards (172) and have over 100 yards receiving (109) in a Rose Bowl game. Overall, he set a new Rose Bowl record with 368 all-purpose yards.

No wonder Christian felt banged up and needed some work.

Christian is one of those rare athletes with both God-given athletic ability and impeccable work ethic. He was driven to do everything he could to improve his performance and perfect his skills. My work with him extended beyond fixing his pain and aligning his body physically, to deeper discussions about how his mind could be his greatest asset or his worst enemy; how his thoughts and behavior could affect his body's ability to heal and perform.

As the 2016 college football season was nearing, Christian asked if I would be willing to come to Stanford on Sundays, the day after their games, to work on him and some selected teammates. I was to provide 30 minute sessions of muscle therapy so they could recover from their injuries.

It was a very exciting time as I, on a weekly basis, worked with young, well-mannered and smart athletes looking for pain relief and seeking to improve their game both physically and mentally to one day play in the NFL.

As I worked with the Stanford athletes, I started to systematically use the ancient Chinese wisdom to explain cause and effect of behavior, beliefs and thoughts in an athlete's performance.

I started to relay how their struggles in healing from an injury, as well as not learning from a disappointing performance, was due to not following the way taught by ancient Chinese masters. My weekly treatment sessions and conversations with Christian and his Stanford teammates conceptualized the book you are now reading, *Athlete's Way of Excellence: Ancient Chinese Secrets to Modern Day Athletic Peak Performance and How to Be in the Zone*.

This simple ancient wisdom, when applied diligently, will improve athletic performance of body and mind. It has been used for thousands of years by Zen monks, Shaolin priests and kung fu grand masters and can still be used today to show the "Way" to master a skill and to perform in excellence.

In the Way of Excellence, every workout, every game, every instance of competition or athletic performance should, in theory, be better than the previous one. If it is not, it means you did not **learn** your lesson from your previous performance, did not fully **recover** (rest and nutrition), were not fully **committed** (desire), were not fully **engaged** or were not **present** in the Zone of your athletic performance. It is amazing how often an athlete is grooming bad habits by repeating a pattern of his athletic performance that is not working. There is cause and effect, action and reaction, meaning and purpose with everything that happens. The simple wisdom from ancient teachings in this book will help you improve your performance and enjoy playing your game.

This book will be of great value to any athlete who is seeking to improve their game and strive for excellence in their athletic pursuit.

The greatest obstacles and battle for you to perform in the Zone is in your own mind.

Ignorance, lack of awareness and knowledge cause repetition of disappointing results.

Insanity is doing the same thing over and expecting a different result.

The information in this book will guide the athlete to be present, at peace and of one mind; free of mental chatter, performance anxiety or regret. The wisdom of this book teaches how to be, what to do and when to do it, always in perfect timing and excellence.

Athlete's Way of Excellence is written for athletes, but the ancient principles of wisdom being taught in this book can be applied for excellence of all things in life. They can be applied to be in excellence as a husband, wife, parent, and friend, as well as excellence in your profession, your career, your health and your fitness.

Contents

CHAPTER 1

Introduction

Perfect timing, being in the Zone, doing the right thing at the right time, is all about being in a state of excellence.

Five-thousand-year-old Chinese wisdom teaches the **way** of how "to be," as well as what and when "to do," in harmony with our surroundings and our circumstances. Those same principles have been used by masters of kung fu and other forms of Asian martial arts for thousands of years. Mastery of this Way of Excellence allows for an effortless going with the flow of what is, regardless of the situation and circumstances at hand.

Bruce Lee, the iconic kung fu martial artist and movie star, made this way of living part of his life with his saying: "Be like the bamboo; bend slightly with the wind and spring back stronger." [1]

The Way of Excellence describes a method to master a skill. This is the ancient practice of kung fu. The original meaning of the word kung fu is made up of two Chinese characters; the first, kung, means skillful work or endeavor and the second, fu means time spent. To practice kung fu in the true meaning is to spend time perfecting a skill. A master of kung fu is one who displays tremendous proficiency in one's craft.

To paraphrase Bruce Lee: "Kung fu is an integral part of the philosophy of Tao and Zen, the ideals of giving with adversity, to bend slightly and then spring up stronger than before, to have patience in all things, to profit by

---

[1] All Bruce Lee quotes excerpted from *The Warrior Within*: The Philosophies of Bruce Lee by John R. Little. This edition published in 2016 by Chartwell Books, an imprint of The Quarto Group, 142 West 36th Street, 4th Floor, New York, NY 10018, USA www.QuartoKnows.com

one's mistakes and lessons in life. These are some of the many aspects of the art of kung fu; it teaches the way to live"

The word "way" has many meanings. In this text it is defined as; how something is done, a method or system that can be used to do something; the course, path or road traveled from one place to another. A course of action, a series of actions or sequence of events leading to a direction or toward an objective, a possible decision, action, or outcome.

Athletic peak performance is brilliant, and it takes place in a state of peace and grace. It is never forced nor tense. It happens automatically without thinking. The individual often states that it felt like time slowed down and all their senses were heightened. The experience is euphoric, and every athlete who has ever experienced this state wants to experience it again. The problem is how do you live and train to reach this stage on a regular basis? How can we sustain this state of excellence for longer periods of time?

Ancient Chinese wisdom teaches four stages of "doing" and one ever-present stage of "being." Those stages of excellence are explained as a metaphor. A metaphor is telling a story using figurative language or symbols. Those four stages, or durations of time, are metaphorically named after the four seasons: spring, summer, fall and winter.

The first stage is "Spring" – a time for **Commitment**. A new beginning, a time to give birth to a dream, realizing a goal, making a decision and committing to a cause of action. The second stage is "Summer" – a time for **Action/Competition**. The action that leads to accomplishment over a period of time with proper repetition. The third stage is "Fall" – the outcome or **Result**. Something that happens as a result of an activity or process. The fourth stage is "Winter" – the **Recovery**. A necessary stage of reflection and recovery before a new cycle of growth can start over.

Each one of those four stages can last for an hour, a day, a week, a month, a year, or *any* duration of time. Hence it is a metaphor of time named after one of the four seasons. Excellence is "doing" the right thing at the proper time (season). Each "season" represents a duration of time doing the "right" thing. Each stage is one of four, all necessary, that make a whole complete cycle of excellence.

The Ancient Chinese also talked about a fifth ever present stage of One-Mindedness. This stage is about "being" of **Present Mind**, calm and at peace in the here and now.

The act of "doing" in each of the four stages of time are explained as a parable. A parable is a short story that teaches a lesson. The parable of the "seed" is teaching us that everything we think, say and do is a "seed planted." Everything we think, say and do has consequences. As we sow, so will we reap. The principle of the seed is to bear fruit and to multiply. This is a universal law that we can be ignorant about, but we cannot escape its consequences. When you plant a seed, you do not get one seed back, instead, you get tenfold or a hundredfold. This is why it is important to plant a good seed to bring forth a great harvest.

The Spring **Commitment** phase represents the beginning with planning and decision making or in other words "planting a seed," making a commitment. The Summer **Action** phase represents activity, labor of love, and joy, or in other words tending to the soil and planted seed by "watering and weeding." The Fall **Result** phase represents the outcome, completion, and closure, something accomplished or learned i.e. "bringing in the harvest." The Winter **Recovery** phase represents experience, reflection, storage, recovery, and rest. All are necessary before you can start over with a new beginning or "Spring."

The ever-present moment is the state of "being" not "doing," to be grounded, calm, and present in the here and now. "Being" of **Present Mind** and at peace in each "season" of "doing." Timing is doing the right thing at the right time. Doing one thing at a time while "being" in excellence.

No one questions the success of the current New England Patriots head coach Bill Belichick. With 15 Division championships, 8 AFC Conference championships and 5 Super Bowl championships in 18 years as a head coach, he has created a dynasty. This was done in an era of the salary cap.

In professional sports, a salary cap is an agreement or rule that places a limit on the amount of money a team can spend on players' salaries. It exists as a per-player limit or a total limit for the team's roster, or both. The salary cap was installed to create a competitive balance in the league. The Patriots became victims of their own success. Their players' value increased to such an amount they could no longer hold onto them all. Every year, the Patriots lost players who were offered more money and bigger contracts by other teams who had not exceeded their cap and could afford them. How could Belichick keep winning and be as successful as he had been when he had to bring in new, less experienced and less expensive players every year?

Belichick is famous for his expression, "**Do your job**." The success of his teams can be summarized by the fact that each and every player knows what their job is and when to do it. Knowing what to do and when to do it is a requirement to be in the Way of Excellence. A team is no stronger than its weakest link. Belichick knows his players' abilities and does not ask or expect them to do more than they can do (doing their best). When they do what he tells them, when he tells them to do it, they are usually successful.

The Way of Excellence is all about timing, doing the right thing at the right time. Even if you are an athlete in an individual sport you still need the knowledge of "how to do your job," knowing what to do and when. In *Athlete's Way of Excellence*, ancient Chinese wisdom is used to metaphorically explain what to do, when to do, and how to be.

Striving to apply the wisdom of the Way of Excellence in your athletic pursuit and everyday life will bring excellence. This book will present **12 lessons** for you to read and practice on your path to excellence. Each lesson teaches mastery of one of the stages.

CHAPTER 2

Patrick Marleau

Photo Credit: © Anne-Marie Sorvin-USA TODAY Sports

I have worked with Patrick Marleau since 2004 and can attest to his impeccable work ethic and constant desire to get better physically and mentally. I consider him a dear friend, and over the years we have read and discussed many books about personal growth and human performance.

Patrick Marleau won gold medals with Team Canada at the 2010 and 2014 Winter Olympics. He was one of the most important players of the Sharks for nearly 20 seasons and exhibits a high standard of playing ability combined with gentlemanly conduct. This has earned him two nominations for the Lady Byng Memorial Trophy and has made him a popular player among fans and his professional peers.

Patty takes excellent care of his body, and at 38 years of age he is still one of the fastest players in the NHL and has a staggering streak of 706 consecutive games played.

- Athlete's Way of Excellence

CHAPTER 3

Christian McCaffrey

Photo Credit: © Greg M. Cooper-USA TODAY Sports

At a young age, Christian is blessed with a God-given athletic talent and has an impeccable work ethic. He is constantly searching for ways to get better both physically and mentally. Desire, commitment, passion, humility, courage, and faith are virtues he displays.

At his first press conference, when introduced as the Carolina Panthers' first pick in the 2017 NFL draft, he told reporters; "When I don't play football, I'm preparing for football."

Christian had learned that the way he eats, breathes, sleeps and thinks at any moment of any day affects his performance on game day.

- Athlete's Way of Excellence

CHAPTER 4

Martin Jones

Photo Credit: © Stan Szeto-USA TODAY Sports

Martin Jones stays calm and present, never gets too high or too low, and is always steady no matter the circumstances. He led the San Jose Sharks all the way to the Stanley Cup final in his first year as a starting goal keeper in the NHL.

Martin is wise to focus only on the things he has control over. He goes about perfecting his skills, profiting from his mistakes by learning and getting better every day.

- Athlete's Way of Excellence

The greatest obstacle and battle for

you to perform in the Zone

is in your own mind.

CHAPTER 5

Karen Chen

Photo Credit: © AP Photo/Jeffrey Phelps

World-class figure skater Karen Chen has the work ethic, discipline, and talent to be successful. At a young age, she learned that her mind could be her greatest asset or her worst liability both when it came to healing from a potentially career-ending injury, as well as performing at the big championships.

In 2017, she "skated out of her mind" when she found the Zone at and won the nationals and came in fourth in her first world championship.

- Athlete's Way of Excellence

CHAPTER 6

Spring - Commitment

In the spring, the farmer spreads manure, collected over the year from his livestock, onto his fields. He turns the soil over and then takes his best seeds and plants them.

LESSONS 1-3

Everyone has a God-given talent, whether you have realized yours or not. This gift is a seed with tremendous potential. What you do with this seed is your gift to the world. What are your goals, dreams, and desires? Do you have a plan? Do you know where you are going? If you don't know where you are going, then you are just aimlessly wandering around. The **COMMITMENT** phase is about planning and getting clear on purpose and direction. It is about finding a cause to commit to.

It's important to get clear on what YOU need, what DRIVES you, and what makes you tick. What makes us do the things we do? What drives us? Why do we even bother to get out of bed in the morning? Even if we don't realize it on a conscious level, we are driven by basic human **needs**. Many of us have been conditioned to believe that being needy or having needs is a negative thing. Yet every action we take and every word we speak is motivated by a need that we want met. Unmet needs can lead to distress, tension, failure, pain, suffering, injury, and over time even disease.

In addition to our needs, we have wants. People often confuse needs with wants. For instance, you may need a car for transportation, but you don't need a Ferrari. Unless you have enough wealth, buying a Ferrari may not bring you peace and satisfaction. What it could do is bring unintended consequences – going deep into debt, worrying about maintenance, being scared to drive it and have it scratched, nicked, damaged, or even stolen. This example could be the root of the famous proverb, "Be careful with what you ask for; you might get it." Think about it. How do you know that what you want is really what's best for you?

We also have **GOALS** and **DREAMS**. A goal is a plan of action for how we can achieve a need or want. A goal is something we believe we can accomplish. Many people are so bent on achieving their goals that they do not enjoy the journey. The journey (being in the moment), not the destination (reaching the goal), will bring you true peace and satisfaction. A dream has no limits, but there is a big difference between having dreams and being a dreamer. Dreams, creativity, and imagination set in motion have given the world some of its greatest athletic performances, discoveries, inventions, and other wonders. If you give up on a dream, a part of you will die.

Our **Desires**, needs, wants, goals and dreams are the fuel that keeps us going. This fuel is what makes us engage in life; it is what's alive in us. Our **desires are the seeds we need to plant to grow**, blossom, and bear fruit. Getting clear on your dreams, goals, and needs is getting clear on what you desire. The stronger the desire, the stronger the seed. Strong desire is what helps the seed grow through times of hardship.

What is the purpose of playing the game? In the Way of Excellence, the true purpose is to have fun competing, to be challenged and get better, to commit to mastery in your athletic endeavor, and to experience excellence. If your desire is strong enough, it can drive you in a lifetime commitment of striving for mastery of your skill or sport.

Lesson 1:

Decide on What to Plant

In accordance with the ancient teachings, the Way of Excellence is about committing to mastery of a cause. This cause could be committing to be the best athlete you can be, committing to master a skill or athletic activity, and realizing that this is a never-ending project.

In the West, we think of a goal as a linear approach and something to reach. Many people are so focused on reaching their goal that they make the present moment nothing more than a means to an end to reach a more important future moment, such as when they "cross the finish line" or reach their goal.

Goals are not always reached – or reached when we expect to reach them. Even if we do reach our goal, if we only live for that moment, we keep being disappointed because life moves on and that moment never lasts. A commitment is ongoing and cyclical, as long as we are still committed to our cause. Every morning is a new beginning to strive for excellence and mastery.

Get clear on and commit to what you desire to master. This desire is your "**seed**" that needs to be **planted** for your excellence, personal satisfaction and peace of mind. If you do not have a commitment or direction, your destination is left to chance instead of intent. Commit to mastery of a specific skill or sport that you desire. Commit to mastery of fitness. Commit to mastery of coaching. Commit to mastery of whatever skill or endeavor you can imagine. Sign a contract with yourself either on paper or in your mind to solidify your commitment.

Making this commitment = planting your seed.

Lesson 2:
Planting Daily Seeds

Every morning is a new day. As you awake, ask yourself if you are still committed to your cause. Then set up goals, or things to do today that will help you grow closer to mastery. Ask "What can I do or visualize today to get closer to mastery of my commitment?" This could be something that takes minutes to hours of your day. It does not necessarily matter how much time you spend each day, as long as you are still committed and still challenge yourself.

There must be a balance between skill and challenge in your everyday goals. If the daily goals or challenges are frequently too high for your current skill, you will become stressed and discouraged. If your daily challenges are frequently too low for your current skill, then you will find yourself bored and lose interest. Try setting the bar at a height where you have a chance to make it, but do not set it so low that it is too easy. Commit to a daily challenge you believe you can reach and not some farfetched "pipe dream." As you, with time, master this process, you will grow in confidence and skill. As your skill grows, your challenge needs to rise. The bigger daily goals you reach, the more you believe in yourself and the greater daily challenges you can take on. A goal is a challenge for growth, a stepping stone and a learning experience. A commitment is a never-ending ongoing process, a lifestyle of excellence.

Every morning as you start your day, write down or mull over what you can do today (daily goal/challenge) to get a step closer to mastery.

Lesson 3:

Cleansing and Fertilization

Every morning when you **recommit** to your cause for the new day, get clear on what has worked and what has not up to this point. Keep doing what brings improvement and growth, and change your approach in everything that does not bring improvement and growth.

Changing the approach is the same as making **game plan adjustments** in a football game when things are not going well. Everyone is still committed to winning the game but the plan on how to win is changing. Compare it to your car's GPS (navigation system). When you stray off the path or make a wrong turn the automated GPS voice tells you, "**Rerouting** your directions!" This is done to assure you get to your destination. To keep going when you can see that you are lost or that things are not working is a waste of time.

Diligently, every day and in every moment, get clear on your purpose, direction, the intent of every action you take, every word you speak, and every thought you think. Every moment is a new beginning, and your thoughts, words or actions are the "seeds" you later will harvest. Make sure all of your actions, words, and thoughts are in alignment with you being in excellence to achieve your daily goals and to get closer to mastery.

Each and every morning we wake to a new day, and every morning we need to get clear and decide if we are still committed to our cause. If we are, then we keep doing and perfecting what works, and we change our game plan when it doesn't.

If one morning we wake up and we are not 100% committed, then we need to cleanse our thinking and change our attitude **or** we need to commit to something else. Continuing to do something without being fully committed is fruitless.

Before you start – every day, every workout, every repetition, every competition – get clear on what you need to do, how you need to be (your attitude and presence), what you need to say and what you need to think to be aligned with getting closer to reaching your daily goals and mastery of your skill or sport.

Aim to make every day, every workout and every effort greater than the previous day. This is how you get better and multiply your "seed" for continued growth and greater harvests.

Get clear on what works – that is, what brings improvement and growth – and what does not. Change what you do when it does not show improvement, and keep doing what brings improvement so that every day you get more efficient to operate in growth and excellence. This might sound obvious, but it is amazing how often athletes keep doing the same thing over and over without getting results. Insanity is doing the same thing over and over when it doesn't work.

Keep a journal of every workout, and write down how you felt and the results.

Communicate, speak up, and be assertive about your needs to coaches and teammates. Tell them what works for you and what does not so that you can be on a path of continuous growth.

If you find yourself stuck, repeating a pattern over and over without getting results (harvest) you are satisfied with, then you are most likely frustrated, irritated and angry at yourself or others around you. This anger can get toxic, as all you think about is what does not work out and what you do not need. The more this pattern is repeated, the more you keep thinking about what you don't need and what doesn't work, the more you will reap of the same outcome. If you keep doing what you have been doing, then you will keep getting what you have been getting.

Since your words, thoughts and actions are "seeds" planted, you will only get more of the same. The mind moves toward whatever you are thinking about. If you, for example, are a golfer or a figure skater and all you can think about is how you mishit the ball or messed up your jump, you will keep doing it. All you can think of is what you do not want. You are unable to think of what you need. Every new attempt is a new commitment, a new seed planted and a new spring.

Whenever you find yourself frustrated, angry or resentful over things not going your way, you need a mental adjustment or cleansing of your "stinking thinking." All your "stinking thinking" – everything that you are frustrated or angry about, everything you do not need – can help you figure out what you *do* need. In other words, "shit" smells, but it helps things grow. Write a list of everything you are frustrated, angry and irritated about with yourself or others around you. In a thesaurus, find the antonyms for everything on your list. Those are the words that are opposite to the words that describe why you are angry. In the thesaurus, pick the antonym that you like the best and make a new list of the converted, fertilized words. Fertilization is when manure (stinking waste) is used to make the soil richer to better support plant growth. This is how bad experiences of the past can help us grow.

Post your list of converted words on your bathroom mirror and every morning and evening when you brush your teeth, recite the words describing what you need. In this way you start to think about and manifest what you need.

Here's what you need to think, speak, and act upon:

• Think about and imagine how you would like to play and perform. Do not allow visions of how you would not like to play or perform to enter your mind.

• Think about what you need, instead of what you don't need.

• Communicate what you need, instead of angrily blaming yourself and others for not having what you need. This will make it more likely that you will obtain what you need.

Every day is a new beginning,
a new day to start fresh and commit
to be in excellence.

CHAPTER 7

Summer – Action/Compete

In the summer, the farmer waters and weeds his fields. He labors in love, as he inspects his fields daily with joy, because he anticipates a rich harvest.

LESSONS 4-5

In the dictionary, the word compete is defined as "to strive for something that is desired."

The Way of Excellence is to compete or strive for mastery in your athletic endeavor. It is not about being perfect, winning or being a master, but rather **striving** for mastery. It is about the journey, not the destination. It is about getting better every step of the way and every day. True joy comes from loving what you do and loving to compete. Be Authentic and Passionate in your pursuit of excellence. Being in excellence will help you win more frequently than the state of not being in excellence. The fact is that you can control being in excellence, but you cannot control winning.

Lesson 4:

Watering the Seed

Once the seed is planted (the commitment is made), the soil needs to be tended by watering and weeding to assure a Harvest/Result of your liking. The **Action/Compete** phase is metaphorically called "Summer." This is the time period between when the **Commitment** was made and the final "outcome" or **Results** are in. The duration of the metaphorical "Summer" can be between seconds to years depending on whether it is a short-term, seasonal, or lifetime goal you are working on. A short-term goal for a golfer could be a single shot on the golf course. The minute between - when he is teeing up the ball, deciding which club to use, and where he wants the ball to land (**Commitment**/"Spring"), the actual mechanics of his stroke and the flight of the ball (**action**/"Summer") until he sees where the ball lands (outcome/**Result**/"Fall"). A seasonal example could be the time from when the football player commits to his seasonal goals (**Commitment**/"Spring"), every individual practice, play, and game (**Action**/"Summer"), until the season's end (outcome/**Result**/"Fall").

The **Action** stage is about your attitude, about laboring in love, about doing what you love or loving what you do. It requires that you enjoy and are engaged, passionate and positive about what you are doing. That you believe in results and succeeding. To be in the Way of Excellence you need to be into, and love, your training as well as the competition. Winners expect to win and love every moment of the competition.

I have seen countless athletes who are suffering from performance pressure at the time of competition. The event or competition makes them tense up and underperform. I ask them why they do their sport, and they all say it is because they love it and it's fun. Then I point out to them that the way they described how they feel when they compete does not sound like they are having fun and love what they are doing. You "play" a sport. The definition of play is the action during a game. Children will stop playing the moment it's not fun anymore. As an athlete, you must always remind yourself that you are playing because it is fun. If you no longer have fun, you need to change your attitude or stop playing.

Brett Favre, the retired hall of fame NFL quarterback, is a perfect example of this. Favre is known as a blue collar player who always remembered to have fun and that he was playing a game, no matter its magnitude.

It's amazing how many athletes have forgotten to have fun, and their playful game has turned into painful labor.

Larger than life personality, 40-year-old Dominican Republic baseball player David Ortiz, nicknamed "Big Papi," is a great example of how performance and excellence will come to full bloom when playing relaxed and having fun. Ortiz's play and performance had been declining over the last couple of years, and he then became a designated hitter and part-time first baseman for the Boston Red Sox. Once Big Papi declared that 2016 would be his last year, he decided to fully enjoy every game and have fun without pressure. In spite of aging and naturally performing at a lower level, to everyone's surprise, his 2016 performance was among the absolute best in the league. Why is it that he could not play relaxed and have fun in prior seasons?

This is clearly a state of mind. When an athlete feels the pressure and the expectations (which is all his perception in his mind), thinks ahead about the outcome of the game, worries about letting others down, or losing a game, then he is no longer having fun or playing in the Zone. The same is true if he is chastising himself, having a hard time accepting his current performance, or that he is aging and slowing down. It is still the same game, and there is no reason to play if you have forgotten that you play to have fun. It would be better if we play every game as if it was our last. Loving what we are doing and having fun. How do we know for a fact, or have control over, how much longer we will play or be active in our sport anyway?

Just because an athlete is having fun competing doesn't mean that he or she has less of a desire to win. We already established that desire has to do with the commitment you already made. At the time of commitment, it's important to get clear on how committed you are, or in other words, how badly you want to reach this goal. The stronger the desire (the planted seed) the greater the will to win. However, it's important while performing your athletic activity to be totally engaged in the Zone and having fun, while loving what you're doing. If you're thinking about the end result (winning or losing), or second guessing while you're in the **Action** phase, then you're not in the Way of Excellence; your mind and body are not 100% engaged in the here and now. The desire to win (Commitment), never stop **Believing, Playing and Competing** until "the last whistle" (**Action**), are the Way of Excellence.

As a matter of fact, it's a waste of time, money and energy to keep working out or competing if you don't have this attitude and state of mind. Such a labor is doomed to be fruitless and not bring a harvest of your liking. If a golfer in the middle of his swing thinks, "Don't hit the ball in the water," he will. The same could be said of the high jumper thinking "I don't think I can make it," as he is running toward the raised bar.

Our Mind Moves Toward Whatever We Focus On

Make sure every word you speak, every thought you think and every action you take is a **positive action** that will help you get closer to reaching your goal. Make sure to socialize with people who are **encouraging** and have a **positive attitude** since this is contagious.

Before you perform your athletic activity (practice or competition), use imagination and visualization to create a virtual reality in your mind to see yourself already performing at the level you desire. Visualize seeing, hearing, and feeling in body and emotions, the entire experience, exactly the way you want it to happen. Pre-play the event over and over. Do this visualization before practice, in between sets or during short breaks. When this is done over and over in hundreds of repetitions, your body will not know if you did this for real or in your imagination. You believe you can do it because you have already done it hundreds of times.

Virtual visualization together with physical practice, done repetitively, will enable you to respond without thinking when you perform your action in competition. In the Way of Excellence, action is a pure state of joy and grace that comes with instinct and muscle memory.

Lesson 5:

Weeding Your Garden

Weeding is the process of eliminating obstacles. Visualize the solution to any obstacle, the answer to any problem. Don't worry about "how" this can happen, just keep visualizing the solutions instead of seeing the problems or obstacles.

The "Summer" or **Action** phase requires **discernment** or weeding; in other words, separate positive from negative, pure from impure, true from false and good from bad. Just like the farmer pulls weeds from his fields to ensure his harvest, our minds, when working in a state of excellence, will discern what serves us and what does not. Your mind is your "garden." You need to keep it free from "weeds." When listening, ask yourself, "is what I hear 100% true? Is it good? Does the information benefit me?" If the answer is not yes to at least one of those three questions, reject the information. Pluck the weed!

When communicating with others, ask yourself the same questions. Is what you intend to speak 100% true? Is it good edifying information? Will it benefit the individual you are communicating with? If the answer is not yes to at least one of those three questions, avoid speaking this information. Obviously, mindless gossip needs to be weeded out. If you can't say anything nice, don't say anything at all.

Avoid socializing with negative people since negativity is a weed that can strangle your harvest. Negativity is like a virus that multiplies and can kill your goals and dreams.

Before taking part of any activity, ask yourself if this activity will bring you joy, if it is good and fruitful, and if it will bring you closer to achieving your goal. If the answer is not yes to at least one and preferably all of the questions, refrain from this activity.

When eating, ask yourself if what you intend to eat is healthy and if it will benefit you and help you reach your goal. Think of food as fuel for performance and mastery rather than temporary pleasure for your taste buds. This weeding or discernment is ongoing and essential or the "weeds" and negativity will strangle your harvest (prevent you from reaching your goal). The act of weeding requires continuous repetition day by day and moment by moment.

Negative thoughts, not being engaged or not fully believing, will guarantee that you will not succeed. It is important to have the right attitude and state of mind in every action, repetition, workout or competition.

See if you can go for an hour, half a day or even a whole day without thinking or speaking negative words or thoughts. Always see "the glass as half full rather than half empty." After all, it is all about your perception and attitude.

Momentum

Your spoken words, thoughts, and actions could be part of the solution or part of the problem. You need to "weed" out/discern all words, thoughts, and actions that are not positive (do not cause joy and blooming). You need to "water" or encourage your belief in a positive outcome ("bountiful harvest"). Momentum is like a boulder rolling down a hill. It picks up speed and becomes an unstoppable force. If you play on a team, you have probably experienced a time when the team believed they were getting stronger and stronger, until as a collective force you all believed you were unstoppable. The compounded action, belief, positive spoken words and thoughts of the entire team feeds the momentum. Momentum also can go the other way. One teammate stops believing and starts to speak and think negatively. Then it spreads from one teammate to another, and another, until the team is defeated. At this point, the teammates no longer believe they can win. Choose to be part of the solution instead of a part of the problem.

CHAPTER 8

Fall - Result

In the fall, the farmer is rewarded for his work as he accepts and receives his harvest. As nature teaches him each year, he learns from his success as well as his failure to improve as a farmer and grow as a man. He accepts the harvest he is dealt and the change of the seasons to move on with ease.

Receiving, Achieving and Learning = **Accepting** the **Result** and **Outcome**

LESSONS 6-7

True satisfaction comes from knowing that you did your best, that you battled and were challenged to learn and grow. This you must accept because it is the only thing you have control over. There are too many circumstances outside your control for you to win all the time. True success is not about being perfect or winning. It is about striving for perfection; know you did your best, that you were challenged, that you learned and grew from the experience. If you always learn from the process, you get a little bit better every day and a lot better with time. Sports has drama; we never know for certain the outcome. That's why we play the game.

The legendary UCLA basketball coach John Wooden (who won 88 consecutive games and ten NCAA championships in a 12-year period, including seven in a row), never once talked to his players about winning. He was meticulous in preparing his players in how to do their job. Coach Wooden had the wisdom to realize that it is impossible to control any circumstance other than every player competing hard and doing their best.

Lesson 6:

Bring in the Harvest

There is always a **Result** or an outcome, therefore there is always a harvest.

It is easy to **accept** the result or outcome when things go your way and you are victorious in reaching your desired goal. To be in the Way of Excellence, it is important to stay humble, gracious and have empathy for your competition. All the circumstances worked out in your favor and it was not all about you. The Way of Excellence makes you realize that your competitions' efforts and disappointments are intimately linked to your success.

Anyone who has lived a little has learned that life does not always happen the way we expected or desired. In the whacky world of sports, you can do everything right and still lose. Another time you can play or compete poorly and still win. Sometimes circumstances emerge that you have no control over: weather conditions, unlucky bounces, referee, umpire or judges' honest errors, superior performance from your competition and many other factors.

Phil Mickelson, in the 2016 British Open, finished with a score 17 under par that would have won almost any previous golf major. The victory was not his since Henrik Stenson finished with an unbelievable 20 shots under par.

In game 6 of the 2008 Stanley Cup conference semifinal between the Dallas Stars and San Jose Sharks, the Sharks did not come out victorious. The game went on to four additional periods of sudden death overtime. The game went on for almost 5 ½ hours and finished at 1:22 a.m. Either team could have won, but margins of seconds, inches and the bounce of the puck determined the outcome. The Sharks goalkeeper Evgeni Nabokov played an outstanding game and had one of the best saves in playoff history, however, history remembers only that Nabokov and the Sharks were losers.

Photo Credit: © LM Otero/ASSOCIATED PRESS

It is possible to be in the Way of Excellence and still lose. Think about this for a moment. Would you rather experience playing, competing and performing at your all-time best in the Zone and lose, or play awful, get lucky and win? When put in this perspective, the definition of winning and losing is not as clear. In other words, it is possible to lose and still perform like a winner, just as it is possible to win and play like a loser.

Accepting the outcome equals reaping a harvest. When things did not go the way you expected and you can't accept the **Results** or outcome, then you are stuck. Everything happens for a reason. Reality is what it is. Not accepting the outcome is arguing with reality. How can you say this is not supposed to happen this way when it just did? The game moves on; life goes on. Second guessing, chastising, or feeling sorry for yourself will not help you learn, grow and move forward.

Accept the fact that you always do your best. This is true unless you deliberately took action to fail. You might believe you could always have done better. You say, "I should have done this or I should have done that." However, wisdom states that we always do the best we can based on the circumstances and resources we have at hand. We always do the best we can based on our state of mind, what we believe, the energy level, knowledge, time and money we have at the time. If you would have realized that you could have done "this" or "that" at the time, then you would have done it. Since you didn't do it you were obviously distracted, had no knowledge of, had forgotten or didn't realize those options at the time.

Think about it, if everything went 100% the way you expected 100% of the time, you would get bored. You would not be challenged, learn or grow and would lose interest in pursuing your sport.

Bruce Lee once said, "A goal is not always meant to be reached, it often serves simply as something to aim at."

If you shoot for the stars and get to the moon, you still got ahead. How do you know you are supposed to reach a goal? Simple, you know it when you reach it. How do you know you are not supposed to reach a goal? When you don't!

It was still a learning experience that challenged your growth, so keep moving forward.

Sports has drama. We never know for certainty the outcome, that's the reason we play the game.

The Way of Excellence is accepting the outcome when things go your way as well as when they don't. It's realizing that it's impossible to fail if you always do your best and always learn from the event. You will always grow and always be a winner if you learn and grow. If you always learn, remember what you learned, and try a new approach, you will by process of elimination get better and better and more likely achieve your goal in the future. In this way, you always will realize a "harvest" or accomplishment even when it is not what you expected. If you always do your best and always learn something then you will get better and better day by day. A "Harvest" can be reaching your goal or understanding, learning and growing in the process to get closer to accomplish the goal in the future.

It is possible to win but act as a loser, as well as lose and act as a winner. In the Way of Excellence, a true winner is humble with empathy in success or defeat. "Showing off is the fool's idea of glory." - Bruce Lee

Lesson 7:

Daily Harvest

DAILY LEARNING THROUGH JOURNALING

Many athletes are perfectionists and very hard on themselves. No matter what is accomplished in a day's work, this individual never has a sense of accomplishment because they always think they should have done better or more.

If this is how you live your life, you would benefit from writing a journal at the end of each day. Write down what you did and what you accomplished and/or learned each and every day. You might say, "I didn't have a good day" or "I didn't learn anything." However, if you look hard and long enough you will see that you always learn something. No matter how insignificant or great a learning experience or accomplishment, write it down. This will be difficult at first since you are so used to focusing on what you didn't do well enough. With your journaling, you realize that you always learn and that failure is only failure if you fail to learn. You will feel a greater sense of accomplishment and self-esteem when you focus on what you learn and keep moving forward.

Commit to writing this journal for 21 consecutive days. By this time, you should realize how this benefits your personal growth. If it proves of great value for you and you are disciplined enough, then it would be good to make this an ongoing habit. Repetition and practice will lead to mastery and excellence, and in time this exercise will build insight, as your lessons build upon one another.

When you believe you must be perfect to be successful then you are never quite good enough and never realize a harvest. This belief is very stressful and exhausting. If you instead believe in giving your absolute best, and realize what you learn will always get you better, then you are indeed successful. Realizing that you always learn will keep you moving forward and therefore always accomplish something. This will help you build skill and self-esteem. If you learn and get a little better every day then you get a lot better over time. On a daily basis tell yourself, "I always do my best based on my circumstances and state of mind; I always learn and grow from the experience." Repeat this affirmation like a mantra, until it is what you believe.

True **satisfaction** comes from knowing that you did your best, battled and were challenged to **learn** and **grow**.

This you must accept because it is the only thing you have control over. There are too many circumstances outside of your control for you to win all the time.

Accept and approve of your efforts, accept that you always did your best, always **learn** from the outcome, remember what you learned and keep changing your approach (game plan) until you get desired **results**.

CHAPTER 9

Winter – Recovery

In the winter, the farmer stores and preserves the excess from his harvest so it will feed him and his family over the cold, unproductive winter. It is a time for maintaining equipment, rest, recuperation, and inward activity.

LESSONS 8-9

Appreciate what you have, respect your limits, be **still** and **rest**. All things in nature need a period of recovery before a new cycle of life and growth can begin.

The Recovery phase is also about **Remembering (storing)** what you learned from your past results so that you can benefit from **experience** gained. What good is it to learn a lesson if you forget it and have to learn it over again?

In our rushed and impatient world, everyone wants instant results: quick money, fast food, and rapid weight loss. But what good is accomplished by gaining prosperity, acquiring new knowledge, or losing excess body fat if we lack the wisdom to manage the money, use the knowledge, or maintain a lean, fit body? What good is it to learn a lesson if we are not able to store and keep what we gained or apply what we learned?

The same is true about relationships – significant others, coaches, trainers, and friends. What good is it to gain those relationships if we fail to keep them? It's about **remembering** what you learned and **appreciating** what you have.

Dissatisfaction with your life and accomplishments, jealousy, restlessness, impatience, never being still, and always looking to move ahead will lead to chronic urgency, anxiety, and lack of peace. An athlete who is never satisfied, cannot be still in body or mind because he is constantly moving and racing, fearful of running out of time or getting behind and frequently overtraining. This fear-driven behavior is reckless to our health because we will not get enough rest, causing constant exhaustion of body and mind with decreased performance followed by lingering injuries.

The most important factor of the "Winter" metaphor is Recovery, and the most important part of Recovery is getting enough **sleep**. A hard-training athlete is like a growing child who needs to have a good eight hours of sleep. It is not only about getting enough hours (quantity) of sleep but also getting quality sleep. All your hard training is for nothing if you don't have enough quality sleep. Do you wake up rested and refreshed or achy and tired? If your body and mind are still tired, then you are not fully recovered. When our body is achy and tired, it means we need to rest. Not listening to your body is like continuing to drive your car while ignoring the warning light on your dashboard that indicates you are low on gas.

A majority of injuries happen in training for a sport when the athlete does not listen to the body's warning signals and pushes through when exhausted or burned out. Ski accidents frequently happen when a person has a ton of fun and says "I'm exhausted," then ignores this and goes for one more run. There are times in competition when it is necessary to push through, but you cannot continue to drain your well on a daily basis in everyday training without ultimately suffering consequences. If you work out when you are exhausted and achy, then you are not fully recovered. This workout will not help you get better, stronger or faster but rather cause further breakdown with possible injury to follow. It is the same as spending more money than you make. You bankrupt your body breaking it down rather that building it up.

All athletic training and all exercises break down muscle cells in our body. If we have good quality and quantity of sleep, nutrition and recovery time between the workouts or athletic activity, the body will repair the broken down muscle cells and build them bigger and stronger than before. This is what is called progressive or anabolic training and the only way we get better, stronger, faster and grow in our performance.

There is a huge misconception among many athletes that "more is better." The fearful athlete is constantly reading what the competition and other athletes are doing and keeps adding to his own training while failing to rest and recover.

Progressive training is based on a balance between breaking down (hard training = stress) and building up (rest, recovery, and nutrition). Hard training/stress, if applied gradually with proper time to recuperate, will help us grow both physically as well as mentally.

I had a patient who competed in the Iron Man triathlon in Hawaii for two straight years. He came to see me for injuries every week, month after month as he continued his training. He was reading how the pros trained and even though he had a full-time job, he followed their rigorous program. One injury followed another. Then one day he told me his career was taking off and he no longer had the time to train full-time for all three disciplines of triathlon (swimming, biking and running). He told me he had already qualified for next year's Iron Man in Hawaii and decided that he would go ahead and compete one last time. But this time he would only bike, run or swim if the weather was nice and he had the time and energy. In all the months leading up to the race, he did not get injured once. He went to Hawaii, ran the race, and had more fun than the previous two years, and to his and everyone else's surprise, he had his fastest time. He was obviously doing too much and was constantly over-trained and injured the previous years.

Recovery for a hard-training athlete also requires the necessity to replenish protein and other nutrients in the daily **diet**. Since hard training breaks down muscle cells and the body needs amino acids (derived from protein) to be able to repair and build muscles, an athlete needs at least one gram of protein per pound of lean body weight. If the athlete is trying to increase muscle size, strength or speed, up to two grams of protein per pound of lean body weight is needed on a daily basis in order to build bigger and stronger muscles.

Proper calm and relaxed diaphragmatic **breathing** for maximum oxygen uptake is also a necessity for full recovery and relaxation. Oxygen is necessary for optimal athletic performance and recovery. The lower lobes of the lungs are responsible for 70% of the oxygen uptake. Only through deep diaphragmatic breathing can an athlete remain calm and maximize his oxygen uptake. Chest or clavicular breathing causes a relative oxygen insufficiency as well as chronic anxiety or nervous energy. This type of inefficient breathing overstimulates the sympathetic or "fight or flight" nervous system with an excess stress hormone response and chronic muscle tension. If a person breathes this way, the majority of the time there will be more breakdown than buildup of the body. Deep, relaxed diaphragmatic breathing stimulates the parasympathetic "rest and recover" nervous response.

Proper **hydration** (drinking a sufficient amount of water) on a daily basis is also required for recovery in an athlete. Dehydration is a condition that occurs when the loss of body fluids exceeds the amount that is taken in. With dehydration, more water is moving out of our cells and bodies than what we take in through drinking. We lose water every day in the form of water vapor in the breath we exhale and in our excreted sweat, urine, and stool. Along with the water, small amounts of salts are also lost. When we lose too much water, our bodies become out of balance or dehydrated. Severe dehydration can lead to death. Ideally, the urine should be clear as water or only have a slight tint of yellow. Urine color may indicate dehydration. If urine is concentrated and deeply yellow or amber, you are most likely dehydrated (one exception could be discolored urine due to vitamin supplements). Dehydration will cause muscle contraction that can lead to cramping. Dehydration will affect the muscle's ability to recover and perform. In general, we all need 2 liters plus another half-liter per hour of vigorous exercise per day.

Many overtrained athletes with overstimulated sympathetic ("fight or flight") nervous systems, fall asleep within a minute because they are exhausted; but because of their inability to **still** their mind, they are not able to go into deep sleep and fully relax. They are light sleepers who keep waking up and do not feel rested in the morning. In the Way of Excellence, the athlete remembers what they learned and appreciates what they have. They know their limits and how to be still to rest and recover.

Lesson 8:

Remember What You Learned and Appreciate What You Have

STORE AND PRESERVE THE HARVEST

For those who have taken into practice to write in a "Daily Harvest" journal from lesson 7, lesson 8 would be to read your own journal from first to current date every night before you go to bed. Reading over and over what you have learned will help you **Remember** what you have learned from your past **Experiences**. Remembering what you have learned will prevent you from repeating some lessons of life all over again.

Be in an Attitude of Gratitude

If you are grateful for what you have in life, you are more likely to get what you need. If you, however, are taking what you have for granted and not showing appreciation, you are more likely to lose what you have. Write down a list of all things you are grateful for. This could be your life, your health, your mind, your talents, your purpose, your profession, your home, your daily food, loved ones, friends, coaches, trainers, your freedom, your country, established wealth, personal belongings or anything else you can think of. While lying in bed at night or before arising from your bed in the morning, recite this list of gratitude to make sure you remember, appreciate and never take anything for granted.

"If you are grateful for what you have, then you will gain what you don't have. If you are ungrateful for what you have, then you will lose what you have gained."

Lesson 9:

Learn How to Quiet and Still the Mind to Improve Quality of Sleep

REST AND RECOVER

Learn how to still the mind and relax the body through diaphragmatic breathing exercises.

This breathing exercise should be done while lying on your back in bed before you fall asleep and in the middle of the night if you wake up and find it hard to fall asleep again. Quieting the mind and relaxing the body will assure a deeper more restful sleep which is necessary for recovery and growth.

It is also recommended that you do this exercise in the morning right after you wake up from your alarm clock and before you jump out of bed to check your cell phone for voicemail, text messages and emails. Performing this breathing exercise before you start your day will create a smooth harmonious transition from rest to work day. By practicing breathing awareness, you will learn how to quiet your mind and relax your body. If you are tired and exhausted, you most likely will fall asleep while you do this breathing exercise.

Place one hand on your chest and the other on your abdomen. When you take a deep breath in, the hand on the abdomen should rise higher than the one on the chest. This ensures that the diaphragm is pulling air into the base of the lungs.

1. Inhale: Take a slow deep breath in through your nose imagining that you are sucking in all the air in the room until your belly and chest blow up like a balloon (without straining).

2. Pause for a second or two of quietness.

3. Exhale: Let the air out slowly through your mouth while counting the seconds in your head. As all the air is released with relaxation, gently contract your abdominal muscles at the end to completely evacuate the remaining air from the lungs. It should take 5-20 seconds to completely exhale. It is important to remember that we deepen our respirations through complete exhalation not by inhaling more air.

4. Pause for a second or two.

Repeat the cycle for a total of 15-25 deep breaths and try to breathe at a slow rate.

The use of the hands on the chest and abdomen are only needed to help you train your breathing. Once you feel comfortable with your ability to breathe into the abdomen, you no longer need to place them there. The idea with consciously practicing deep breathing is to reboot your relax/recover (parasympathetic) nervous system and to turn off your fight or flight (sympathetic) nervous system. This is of great value for anyone who has an over-stimulated mind and body and does not know how to be still and relax. At first, you may find that your thoughts jump (your mind drifts) in the middle of your breathing exercises, but as you keep focusing on your breath and practicing mindful awareness, you will be able to take more breaths without having your mind drift. With time and practice, you will be able to get deeper sleep and wake up fresh and relaxed.

What good is there to learn a lesson if we fail

to remember and apply what we learned?

What good is there to train harder if we don't

fully recover before we train again?

CHAPTER 10

Present Mind

Timing is doing the right thing at the right time while "**being**" of one mind, of being in the **here and now**. As the ancient Chinese philosopher, Lao Tzu so simply put it, "**The way to do, is to be**." This means that you are at **peace** and completely **present** while doing one thing at a time. To be in the Zone is the art of "being" rather than "doing." It is a state when the athlete responds and creates automatically, on instinct, or through muscle memory without thinking. It is like being on autopilot.

The Zone is when you are being intensely aware of what you are doing in that instant.

We live in a time when people believe multi-tasking is a skill to be proud of. However, it is impossible to do two or more things at the same time and do it with excellence and at peace. Doing something at 100% requires complete presence and attention.

Anything you have ever done with excellence was done paying attention to nothing but that ONE thing. An athlete performing in the Zone is present and engaged 100% in what he or she is doing. When you are creative or realize a brilliant idea, you are in the Zone. Being awestruck by beauty in nature, art or music is a moment of being present, a moment of excellence. When you are making love you are present and think about nothing but what is experienced in that moment. If you are not present while making love, having a drifting mind, then the experience is not very good.

The Zone is a space where time and self does not exist. In the Zone, one is carefree of pressure from expectations. The moment your ego mind starts to focus on how you are doing or being perceived instead of being completely present in what you are doing, you are no longer in the Zone. The Zone is a state when you are going with the flow or circumstances at hand to operate in excellence. You are not chasing the game, you let the game come to you. You are not separate from the game or your opponent, you rather become one with the whole experience. The ancient Chinese masters called this **wu-shin**, the letting go of self-consciousness and excessive mind activity. Letting go of the nervous, excessive, never ending chatter in your head. This state of mind is when you are thinking too much and trying too hard. You may be upset about what already happened (past) or worry about the outcome (future) which means you are not present in the now. The Way of Excellence and being in the Zone can only happen in the present moment. When you are in the Zone you are not thinking of winning or losing, just being one with your performance in this moment. Wu-shin; to operate free of the excessive chatter in your mind is also referred to as **no-mindedness**. To be in this state of "no mind," you need to empty your mind and become one with the present moment and the circumstances at hand. Bruce Lee explained this with his famous statement "Be like water, my friend." Be formless; be shapeless like water. Water goes around obstacles; it can seep through a tiny crack in a solid concrete wall. Water can be soft and elusive, or it can be hard and crash. Water flows with adversity until it overcomes.

The lack of peace of mind, constant multitasking, and elevated stress levels in today's Western society has led to an increasing interest of ancient Eastern philosophies as well as the practice of yoga, meditation and Tai Chi. The popular term used in our culture for cultivating awareness of the present state of mind is mindfulness. This term – which means being mindful of your present moment, your thoughts and breathing – is in my opinion not a fitting description for a state where you need to quiet or empty your mind. It could be misperceived as striving to have a full mind when the opposite is what is what you desire. This is one of many ways ancient Chinese concepts are misinterpreted by Westerners. Nevertheless, it is encouraging that there is an awakened interest in finding peace of mind since this is a way of improving quality of life and human performance.

The Way of Excellence is going with the flow of things, dealing only with what is in your control in the present moment, having awareness if you need to commit to something, engaging whole heartedly in your activity, accepting and learning from an outcome or remembering and applying what you learned, and lastly, resting and recovering.

Present Mind in the Commitment Phase

Awareness and being completely present is needed when getting clear on purpose and intent for whatever you are to say or do. Having the awareness and being present is necessary to know when to plan or make a decision, as well as to have the clarity on what decision to make. Having the awareness of when to change an approach that did not work ("fertilize") as well as having the awareness of when to commit ("plant a new seed") is necessary for continual growth. Procrastinating making a decision will lead to missed opportunities for excellence and growth. Rushing a decision or commitment before you are ready or clear on what you need will lead to results ("harvest") you don't approve of. This could be likened to "forcing a square peg into a round hole" or trying to "plant seeds in a frozen ground." To be in excellence requires being calm, present, clear and assertive in a time of decision or commitment-making.

Present Mind in the Action/Compete Phase

Being present, engaged, enjoying what you do and being positive is necessary for any activity to be fruitful and to bring results ("harvest") of your liking. This requires awareness of your state of mind in every repetition, every training session, and every competition. Your training and athletic performance needs to be a labor of love and joy, of being present in loving the game and loving to compete, of being present and aware of your thoughts and words, to weed out the negative and water the positive. Being present and authentically engaged is necessary to be in the Zone and perform in excellence. It is not the time to second-guess a decision already made or worry about the outcome once you've started. A pitcher who second guesses his choice of a pitch in the middle of his wind up or worries about serving up a home run is not present in his action. In any athletic action, being present, engaged, and of one mind, is a positive state of joy and excellence.

Present Mind in the Result Phase

Once an activity or action comes to an end, there will be a result or outcome of what you just performed. Like it or not, the outcome may not always be what you expected or desired. This is not the time to second-guess, regret or have remorse over your past actions or commitments; neither is it a time to act as a victim (blaming others) or being a martyr (beating yourself up). For the athlete in excellence, it is a time to be present and accept the outcome, learn from the experience and move on. Surely you never intended to cause yourself or your team grief or disappointment, so as we established earlier, you did the best you could based on what you believed and knew at the time, your state of mind, and your circumstances. If you always do your best and you always realize what you learned, then you are able to move on and grow. Being humble and having empathy in victory or defeat is the Way of Excellence. You can be stuck not accepting the outcome, but life moves on and nothing will change. Whatever just happened, you can learn and grow from it or you can argue with reality refusing to accept what happened only to bring pain and tension to your body and mind.

Present Mind in the Recovery Phase

If you can't let go and move on from what happened, it will affect your ability to rest and recover in peace. Dwelling on what you should have done, how something should not have happened or is not fair, will affect your ability to get good quantity and quality of sleep for full recovery. If this becomes a pattern, lack of quality sleep affects your ability to grow and be successful in the future. Bedtime is not a time to dwell on the past, neither is it a time to start planning, making decisions or worrying for tomorrow.

Being present means awareness, and the easiest way to find awareness is through the breath. By developing an awareness of your breathing, you can control each individual breath to be fully present in this moment. Controlling the breath you are taking right now is controlling the only thing you have any control over – this moment. You could take a deep, slow, relaxed, diaphragmatic breath and feel calm, present, and in harmony. The longer you maintain relaxed deep breathing, the more present and peaceful you will be.

Breathing affects your emotions as well. If you breathe shallowly, take fast breaths, or hold your breath, you will experience anxiety or depression. Anxiety is defined as nervousness about things that have yet not happened, not being present. If you worry about things ahead and feel anxious, your breathing will be shallow and fast.

Depression is defined as being upset about something that already happened, another form of not being present. If you breathe shallowly or hold your breath, you are holding onto the past and most likely harboring upset emotions about something that already happened.

In both cases, the future and the past are things we do not have any control over. The only way we can perform in the Zone, have constructive thoughts, be creative, feel calm, and be at peace, is when we are present. The only way to be present is to breathe deep, slow, relaxed, diaphragmatic breathing. Unfortunately, the most common behavior under stress is one that does not serve us – holding our breath or quick shallow breathing is associated with stress and fight or flight response. If instead, we were present and calm with relaxed breathing, our body and brain would be fully oxygenated and energized to perform under any circumstance at levels beyond what we could imagine. Poor breathing causes oxygen deprivation, negative emotions, and tension, which affect our ability to perform to our maximum capacity both in body and mind. If you've ever watched a tied basketball game go down to the last seconds, the team with the ball will often call a time-out. This allows everyone to take a deep breath, get present, and get clear on a play and a strategy. This is done so that the opportunity to win the game is not wasted by stressed-out players running up the floor like chickens without heads not knowing what to do with the ball. Anytime you find yourself in a stressful situation, you can call a time out in your own head. This awareness will allow you to take a couple of deep breaths, get calm and clear about what you can do, and have control over right here and right now.

Another form of awareness is posture awareness. Bad posture affects the breathing and breathing affects your posture. In fact, it is impossible to slouch and breathe deep, slow, relaxed, diaphragmatic breaths at the same time. Try it for yourself. Close your eyes and perform three or four deep, slow, relaxed breaths. Pay attention to how your posture changes automatically. To breathe correctly, you relax your shoulders, let them move back and drop down. You bring your head back, straighten your neck, and open your chest. When you are breathing incorrectly, you are using muscles in your rib cage and neck to breathe, or not using any muscles by holding your breath. This inefficient breathing does not provide your muscles and brain with enough oxygen, causing your muscles to contract, your mind to tense, and your emotions to be stressful.

In body language, an erect posture with the chest and head high and shoulders relaxed is the posture of a winner. Slouched over with forward head and rounded shoulders are the posture of a defeated loser. Tense, elevated shoulders are the posture of someone who is fearful, anxious or angry. Just as a predator can smell weakness in its prey, your opponent can tell if you are giving up or are afraid by observing your posture.

The final awareness to cultivate is emotional awareness. Your emotions affect your posture and your posture affects your emotions. Likewise, your emotions affect your breathing and your breathing affects your emotions. When you see someone who is depressed, unassertive, melancholic, apathetic, or careless, their posture looks defeated and slouched forward. When you see someone who is anxious, angry, frenzied, grieving, or fearful, they carry tension in their neck and raise their shoulders. When you are present, confident, at peace, calm, assertive, in joy, engaged, passionate, empathetic, still, courageous and careful, your posture will be erect, and your breathing will be deep and calm.

Whenever you are aware of negative emotions or excessive mental chatter in yourself, you can restore peace of mind with one deep diaphragmatic breath.

Breathing

The following information about breathing are excerpts from the book; "Integrative Medicine" by Dr. David Rakel.

Breathing as a Bridge

It is thought by many cultures that the process of breathing is the essence of being. A rhythmic process of expansion and contraction, breathing is one example of the consistent polarity we see in nature such as night and day, wake and sleep, seasonal growth and decay and ultimately life and death. In yoga, the breath is known as prana or a universal energy that can be used to find a balance between the body-mind, the conscious-unconscious, and the sympathetic- parasympathetic nervous system. Unlike other bodily functions, the breath is easily used to communicate between these systems, which gives us an excellent tool to help facilitate positive change. It is the only bodily function that we do both voluntarily and involuntarily. We can consciously use breathing to influence the involuntary (sympathetic nervous system) that regulates blood pressure, heart rate, circulation, digestion and many other bodily functions. Pranayama is a yoga practice that literally means the control of life or energy. It uses breathing techniques to change subtle energies within the body for health and well-being. Breathing exercises can act as a bridge into those functions of the body of which we generally do not have conscious control.

An Example of How Breathing Affects Physiology

During times of emotional stress, our sympathetic nervous system is stimulated and affects a number of physical responses. Our heart rate rises, we perspire, our muscles tense and our breathing becomes rapid and shallow. If this process happens over a long period of time, the sympathetic nervous system becomes overstimulated leading to an imbalance that can affect our physical health resulting in inflammation, high blood pressure and muscle pain to name a few.

Consciously slowing our heart rate, decreasing perspiration and relaxing muscles is more difficult than simply slowing and deepening breathing. The breath can be used to directly influence these stressful changes causing a direct stimulation of the parasympathetic nervous system resulting in relaxation and a reversal of the changes seen with the stimulation of the sympathetic nervous system. We can see how our bodies know to do this naturally when we take a deep breath or sigh when a stress is relieved.

The Breathing Process Can Be Trained

Breathing can be trained for both positive and negative influences on health. Chronic stress can lead to a restriction of the connective and muscular tissue in the chest resulting in a decreased range of motion of the chest wall. Due to rapid more shallow breathing, the chest does not expand as much as it would with slower deeper breaths and much of the air exchange occurs at the top of the lung tissue towards the head. This results in "chest" breathing. You can see if you are a chest breather by placing your right hand on your chest and your left hand on your abdomen. As you breathe, see which hand rises more. If your right hand rises more, you are a chest breather. If your left hand rises more, you are an abdomen breather.

Chest breathing is inefficient because the greatest amount of blood flow occurs in the lower lobes of the lungs, areas that have limited air expansion in chest breathers. Rapid, shallow, chest breathing results in less oxygen transfer to the blood and subsequent poor delivery of nutrients to the tissues. The good news is that similar to learning to play an instrument or riding a bike, you can train the body to improve its breathing technique. With regular practice, you will breathe from the abdomen most of the time, even while asleep.

The Benefits of Abdominal Breathing

Abdominal breathing is also known as diaphragmatic breathing. The diaphragm is a large muscle located between the chest and the abdomen. When it contracts it is forced downward causing the abdomen to expand. This causes a negative pressure within the chest forcing air into the lungs. The negative pressure also pulls blood into the chest improving the venous return to the heart. This leads to improved stamina in both disease and athletic activity. Like blood, the flow of lymph, which is rich in immune cells, is also improved. By expanding the lung's air pockets and improving the flow of blood and lymph, abdominal breathing also helps prevent infection of the lung and other tissues. But most of all it is an excellent tool to stimulate the relaxation response that results in less tension and an overall sense of well-being."

This excerpt was published in *Integrative Medicine* by Dr. Rakel, in the chapter titled "Breathing," pages 693-694, copyright Elsevier, 2003 with permission to use.

In ancient martial arts, masters in kung-fu and karate have long known that staying relaxed by breathing deep and slow in the most intense combat will allow the practitioner to reach a higher state of mind and body. In this state, everything is effortless, as if everything around the individual is moving in slow motion and he has all the time in the world. His mind is quick and creative. His muscles are powerful, and his reflexes react with the speed of light. We have all experienced this effortlessness at one time or another: a time when our mind was limitless, a time when we stopped thinking and just became what we did, a time when out of nowhere we got great ideas or created something beautiful, a time when our bodies performed with ease as if on autopilot. In sports, this state of body and mind is referred to as being "in the Zone." I call it being present, and mastery of this ancient wisdom is striving to experience this state as often as possible and for durations as long as possible.

Your breathing, your posture, and your emotions all provide you with feedback to internally monitor if your body and mind are in balance or not. Once you have awareness of this, you can begin to use it to your advantage by correcting your breathing and posture. You can start to question why your emotions are negative. What are you doing or not doing? Are you present or is your mind drifting or multi-tasking? Are you stuck in a "season" repeating a pattern that is not working? Are you out of balance in the "Commitment," "Action," "Result" or "Recovery" phase?

You can start to question if your thoughts and belief systems are stressful and if they serve you or not. The only reason you experience stress is because you strayed away from the Way of Excellence. Are you believing and dwelling on stressful thoughts in your mind? You can bring awareness to what you think, say, or do and the consequences that follow. You can question if what your mind perceives as stressful is true and real or not. When you manage to stay calm, peaceful, and present, you can stay grounded no matter what external circumstances you are in. Practice being aware and present in each and every moment of your day and athletic pursuit. With proper posture and relaxed deep breathing, your body and mind can perform beyond your greatest imaginations.

A Complete Cycle

A pitcher **decides** on what pitch to throw and **Commits** to it. He is calm, clear and assertive in his Spring phase. He throws the pitch (**Action**) while being calm, present in the Zone and 100% engaged in his Summer phase. The **Result** is either a strike, a ball or a hit. Of course, his intention is never to throw a ball or allow a hit. If the result is not what he expected, he needs to focus on what he learned. He needs to **accept** and learn from the outcome with empathy or humility in his Fall phase. Regardless if the outcome was what he had desired or not, he needs to take a deep breath and **reflect** on what he learned (Recovery) in his Winter phase. If he threw a strike, he may **Commit** to the same pitch as his next one. If he, on the other hand, threw a ball or allowed for a hit, he needs to **Remember** what he learned and change his approach (**Fertilize**) before he **Commits** to his next pitch in the next

Spring phase. In all of those steps, he remains present, going with the flow and being calm in the here and now, thinking about nothing but what he is to do in each instance, being of **One Mind**. This assures that he is in the Zone.

The purpose of the seed is to multiply and bear fruit. Following those ancient principles, the longer we practice the better we get. In this way, we better the seed we plant and improve our **Results** (multiply our harvest).

As you practice and begin to master this Way of Excellence, you will realize that it is not the destination but rather the journey itself that is of importance. A thousand-mile journey starts with one step, and most importantly, the only thing you have any control over is always the quality of the step you take right NOW.

Lesson 10

One Breath Mini Meditation

A TIME OUT TO GET CALM AND PRESENT

This exercise consists of one single breath. The individual pays 100% attention to one breath. Breathe in through the nose and out through the mouth. Hear and feel the air completely filling up the abdomen and the lungs, holding for a second or two and then slowly, completely, deflating the abdomen and lungs. Visualize the image of air completely filling up (inflating) and going out of (deflating) a balloon. This will cause a pause in an overwhelmed mind that was racing with stressful thoughts. Complete awareness of a single breath will bring a moment of being completely present. Not paying attention to your thoughts, but rather bringing the attention back to the breath, will bring peace and a connection with the true self that is not your thoughts.

This breathing exercise could be repeated whenever you experience stress or tension. It is a way to reboot the parasympathetic (relaxing) nervous system, a way to get a present mind, a state where you can create outside the box and perform in excellence.

When things seem to be out of control, you need to be like the center of a wheel. The pin in the center of the wheel does not move regardless of if the wheel is moving slowly or spinning seemingly out of control. This is the same as being still in the midst of a storm. When your life situation seems to be "storming" or "spinning out of control," when you feel overwhelmed, take one deep diaphragmatic breath to calm and center yourself. Then calmly ask yourself what you have control over in this very instant. If you don't have control of anything in that moment then be still until you do. If you have control over a lot of things in that moment, then ask yourself what is of highest priority and then do ONLY that while being calm in excellence. In this way you do one thing, one breath at a time, in excellence.

With practice, one deep breath can instantly put you in the Zone. If you've ever seen a martial arts movie with a master of kung fu, then you have seen how he always takes a deep breath before engaging in combat. This will quiet his mind and center him to enter the Zone.

Lesson 11

A Wake-Up Call to Get Present

If you studied psychology in school, you've probably heard of Pavlov's dogs. Ivan Pavlov was a Russian scientist who discovered a conditioned response in dogs to a repeated stimulus. He found that if he rang a bell simultaneously as he fed his dogs, he created a conditioned response. After this was repeated a few times, the dogs associated the sound of the ringing bell with food. At this point, the dogs would start to salivate when the bell was rung, even if they did not smell or see their food. Thanks to Pavlov's discovery, classic conditioning became the basis for Behaviorism, a school of psychology.

It is interesting to note, that we as humans have conditioned ourselves to behave in certain ways due to various conditioned stimuli. Not presently aware, we subconsciously react to situations we previously experienced as stressful. For the athlete, this could be anything – an event, a location, other people's facial expressions, memories of songs played on the radio, a certain smell, and much more. Everything we perceive is compared to our past experiences or conditioning and judged as good or bad, hence our reaction. All of those conditioned stimuli are what make us feel the way we do. The problem is that so many of those subconscious conditioning stimuli are perceived as stressful or bad when in fact, they may be harmless. Stress is either real or perceived, but even when the danger is not real it is still perceived as real.

As cell phones became more mainstream, I found that they were a cause of negative conditioned response in most of my patients. When I was working on a patient and their cell phone vibrated or rang, I could feel an immediate tightening of the muscle I was working on. This was more noticeable in overwhelmed patients who were under stress. Those were patients who believed they had too much to do and not enough time, and each ring of their cell phone caused more tension in their muscles.

In a time and society where many perceive so much stress and live with an overstimulated fight or flight nervous system, we need to find a way to condition ourselves to be calm, present and in the Zone. Stress is mostly perceived and mostly about the future (things that have not happened yet) and the past (things that have already happened). This takes us away from experiencing the present moment calmly and from doing one thing at a time while realizing that everything is okay right now. Every time we are not present, calm and at peace, we are not breathing right and not performing at our best.

The problem is that we don't know when we're not present because when we realize we're not present, that's when we ARE present. When we realize we're not breathing right, we become present and immediately start to breathe right. When we DO catch ourselves not being present, were we not present for three minutes or an hour? Many people spend most of their day not being present, hence never having peace of mind. It is, however, ONLY when we are present that we can operate in excellence, create and love. Needless to say, life would be lived more fully and we would perform in excellence if we could increase the time of being present in our daily lives. In other words, it would be good if we could have a form of wake-up call to help us get present when we are not. We need to create a new positive conditioning response that will help us get peace of mind.

First, pick a new ringtone for your cell phone, one you have never used or associate with someone or something else. This needs to be a pleasant, non-abrasive ring tone like soft chimes or a bell. When you hear this new ringtone, immediately take one deep diaphragmatic breath before you look at your phone or do anything else. Do this EVERY SINGLE TIME you hear it ring. In this way, you will condition yourself to get present, calm and at peace every time your phone signals you have a call, text message or email. The beauty of this is that the ringing is random and most likely will catch you at a moment when you are not present, not breathing right and experiencing stress. If for any reason, at any time, you cannot commit to take a deep breath when your phone rings, you should turn the volume off ahead of time. For this conditioning to work, it requires a new peaceful ringtone AND that you take a deep breath EVERY TIME it rings. If you apply this lesson to your life and take a deep breath every time your phone rings, you will create more and more moments of calm, present peace. This conditioning will help you get and stay in the Zone more frequently and for longer durations.

The Way of Excellence is Always the Present Moment, Never the Past or the Future

If you are under a lot of stress, overwhelmed and feel you have too much to do and not enough time, you can say an affirmation (quietly in your head or out loud) when your new ringtone goes off and you are taking your deep breath. One of the following affirmations might work for you: "I am calm and at peace"; "I have all the time I need"; or "I create what I need." Repeat this affirmation as a mantra until you start to believe and behave as if it is true.

Lesson 12

Doing One Thing at a Time in Excellence – Stop Multitasking

To be in the Way of Excellence, you need to do one thing at a time. You need to be calm and present at all times under any circumstance. The problem that arises is that we are completely unaware of when we are not present. When we are overwhelmed, our mind is drifting here, there and everywhere. However, the moment we recognize this pattern of not being calm and present in ourselves, we instantly become present. This awareness principle is based on two key concepts:

1. Take note when your mind is wandering away from being in the present moment (the task at hand), you are bored or overwhelmed, disappointed/depressed or worried/anxious.

2. Enhance the present moment through awareness of your breathing. One deep breath will still your mind and clear your thoughts on what you have control over and what is your priority. Then you take action in a calm state of mind. This is the Way of Excellence.

The quicker you catch yourself not being present, the faster you will be able to bring yourself back to the present moment. And because of this practice, you will find yourself being present, calm, and at peace for longer durations.

To demonstrate this principle, here is an example: One day, you find you are overwhelmed, and your mind is racing all over the place. Your mind is frantically screaming, "I have twenty things that need to be dealt with and taken care of right now!" Everyone can easily agree that this state of mind is not harmonious, healthy, productive, or creative. Now, following the principles above, you can take a breathing time-out and ask yourself, "Which of all those things do I really have control over right now?" Not tomorrow or an hour from now, but RIGHT NOW! Taking a deep breath, you can say to yourself, "Okay, I can control those five things." Taking another deep breath, you can ask yourself, "Which of those five things are a priority?" Take another deep breath and say, "Okay those three things." Taking another deep breath you can ask yourself, "Now of those three things, which one of those is the highest priority?" After yet another deep breath, you have successfully identified the number one priority and can say to yourself, "This is the number one priority that I have control over right now!" Good! Do that one thing right now, and do not think about the other nineteen things. Simple, right?

You also can use a positive affirmation to change your belief from, "I have too many things going on right now" to "I always have only one thing to do." There is only one thing that you have control over and at the same time, is the number one priority at any given moment. Do this one thing in excellence.

These exercises and examples show you how you stay calm and present in the midst of stressful circumstances: one thing at a time, one breath at a time. You are only one person, and you can only do one thing at peace and with excellence at any given moment. Resist the urge to say, "I am so busy. I don't have time to do my breathing." In fact, the opposite is true. The more stressed and the busier you are the more important it is to breathe and do one thing at a time.

CHAPTER 11

Positive Affirmations

USE AFFIRMATIONS TO CHANGE YOUR THINKING

If you look back at your experience and behavior in your life up to this point, your behavior was based on habits and beliefs – in other words, what you believed was true at that time. But was this really the truth? If so, then you're doomed to stay right where you are, happy or not. Thankfully, habits and beliefs can all be changed.

I used to be skeptical about affirmations as something "New Age" and lacking substance, like wishful thinking. Then as I continued to live and study on my journey, I realized that all of us, me included, have this voice in our heads that constantly judges us. If you right now are thinking to yourself, "I don't have a voice in my head," that's the voice I am talking about! That voice can run amok and repetitively keep stating a negative affirmation in our heads, over and over until we believe it to be true. Your voice may say things like, "I'm not good enough," "I will never make it," "I am stupid," "I am a loser," "I always get injured," "I am soft," "I am fat or ugly, nobody likes me," or "I always cave under pressure."

We have, in fact, been brainwashed by our own minds to believe in limiting thoughts and untrue beliefs. Move toward what our minds dwell upon and those repetitive negative thoughts become a belief system that does not serve us. Then those belief systems become self-fulfilling prophecies, so we keep repeating the same pattern to confirm that the voices in our heads were right all along. When we recognize and understand this dysfunction of our minds, we can determine which beliefs serve us and which do not.

You may realize quite a few negative beliefs of your own when reading this. The Way of Excellence is having the awareness of our own destructive thoughts and realizing the harm those thoughts will have if we dwell on them. Once we realize destructive negative thoughts, we can then start to use positive affirmations to change (reprograming) a behavior, belief, or habit to something that will serve us.

Affirmations are statements asserting the existence or truth of something. Said over and over again habitually, they can change your interior dialogue from that defeated voice to an uplifting, empowered one. Affirmations should be stated as if they are already true. An affirmation needs to state the positive. For example, "I always win or learn, therefore I always win." Do not use the words "not" or "never" in front of a negative word. An example of how not to use an affirmation would be, "I never lose." Repeating the word "lose" over and over will cause you to lose. We need to repeat a positive affirmation until we start to believe it to be true and start to act in a way that serves us. For example, using the affirmation, "If I always learn, I always win" would reaffirm a positive statement. Look at the suggested affirmations for each of the four phases of excellence below, then choose a few to start changing your behavior, beliefs, and habits.

Spring Affirmations - Commitment

- I know exactly where I am going and what I need.
- I keep changing my approach to improve and grow.
- I am clear on my purpose, direction, desire and goals.
- My desire is strong, and I always overcome.
- My actions, thoughts, and words are my "seeds." I only plant good seeds.

Summer Affirmations - Action/Compete

- I see myself succeed.
- I love what I do, I do what I love.

- I love to perform at _____(the big stage when all the lights are on).
- I am so excited to compete at _____(the main event).
- Everything always works out.

Fall Affirmations - Result

- I always do my best; I always learn and get better every day.
- I always win or learn, therefore I always win.
- I accept what is. Everything happens for a reason; I learn from all life experiences.
- I am worthy of and open to receive all good things.
- There are no mistakes only learning opportunities.

Winter Affirmations - Recovery

- (When tired and achy). I rest when I need to.
- I sleep deeply in peace.
- Everything that is supposed to happen will happen when it is supposed to happen.
- I trust sleep and rest will help me recover and get ahead.
- I am still, like clear water.

Present Moment – Present Mind Affirmations

- I am present, calm and at peace in the here and now.
- I always have what I need when I need it. I create what I need.
- I only have one thing to do at any given moment.
- I have all the time I need.
- I take one deep breath, and I am instantly calm.
- I crave food that builds me up and helps me perform better.

It's quite possible that the affirmation you need the most will sound like a complete lie to you at first. This is because the negative programming has been repeated so many times for so long. Your mind may not accept the positive affirmation as truth, but with time and repetition, the new affirmation will ring truer and truer.

Choose one or two affirmations you think you need the most. Repeat it, or them, in your mind once every hour of the day. Also, every time you're in front of a mirror, look yourself in the eye and repeat the positive affirmation in your mind or out loud. Do this for twenty-one days to form new habits. After the twenty-one days, continue to repeat this positive affirmation (watering) every time the old, destructive belief pops up (weeding).

This might sound like a lot of work but will get easier once it becomes a habit. Just like learning to drive a car with manual transmission might have seemed overwhelming at first, eventually it becomes second nature. Your habits and behavior will gradually change, and your mind will serve you instead of bringing you down.

Virtues of the "Way of Excellence"

Commitment: Desire, integrity, responsibility, honesty
-As you sow, so shall you reap.

Action/Competition: Authentic joy, love (for the game) and passion (for your sport), discernment (positive from negative), diligent persistence
-If you believe you can or can't succeed, you are right either way.

Result: Humility, empathy, understanding, maturity
-The only failure is failure to learn.

Recovery: Gratitude, courage, wisdom, faith
-Knowing is not enough, you must apply what you have learned – Bruce Lee

Present Moment: One thing, one breath at a time, calm and peace of mind -The way to Do is to Be. – Lao Tzu

With this knowledge, you can determine what virtues you lack and need to cultivate to be in excellence.

The Way of Excellence is having the awareness of our own destructive thoughts and realizing the harm those thoughts will have if we dwell on them.

CHAPTER 12

Manage Your Mind

ONE SEASON AT A TIME, ONE MOMENT AT A TIME

Your mind can be your greatest asset or your worst enemy. We have often been told that our minds have potential beyond what we can ever imagine. On the other hand, our minds also can be self-destructive. If your thoughts, beliefs, and interpretation of life are stressful, then your life is a living nightmare. Only when we are calm and present can we be connected with a limitless, creative ability that many (me included) know as God, the One Consciousness, our unlimited source and origin.

You control your own mind, even if you choose to be controlled by someone or something else. All your actions and simultaneous emotional feedback are the result of your thoughts. Your negative, stressful emotions are an alarm clock telling you to wake up, get present, clear, and manage your mind by questioning whether your thoughts are true and serve you or not. As Byron Katie wrote in her book, A Thousand Names for Joy, things are not as they appear. Imagine you're walking down a trail and see a snake just a foot in front of you. Terrified, your heart pounding, you can't move. Then the clouds clear, and the sun shines brighter. In a different light, you see it was not a snake at all, but just an old rope. Now you are laughing and relaxed. You can stand over that rope for a hundred years, and you can't make yourself be terrified by it again. With a calm, present, open mind and some imagination, every stressful thought can be seen in a different light.

The first step is making changes in your thinking and behavior so that you can make every day better than the previous one. The only reason you suffer is because you believe in a stressful thought. But what if you found that the thought was not true? The balanced mind is ever present, ever calm, and has the ability to imagine and create. This mind does not get "stuck" believing stressful, limiting thoughts. This mind is free; it goes "outside the box." If you can be aware of each present thought in each life situation (commitment, action, result and recovery), then you can question if your thoughts are really true or not and then choose an action that will serve you.

Commitment – Spring: Clarity of the Mind, Our Needs, and Our Direction

Every thought is a seed and a new beginning. Is it a good seed that will bring positive emotions and good fruit? Or is it a bad seed that will bring stressful feelings, negative emotions, and suffering? Only you can determine if your thought or perception of something is stressful or not. This requires a clear, honest, and present state of mind.

Seeing a stressful thought in a different light or questioning it from a different perspective can remove your stress and tension as well as change your emotions. What if you looked at every "snake" as a rope? What if you believed that all "crap" can bring something good? Think about your own life. How many times did you perceive that something bad had occurred only to later realize that this "bad" thing had to happen for something better to grow out of it? Certainly, stinking, toxic manure seems bad, but it can become the fertilizer that will bring a greater crop in the future. Everything that happened in the past brings something good; experience helps us gain clarity on what we really want and what is really important. It helps us see what did or did not work so we can keep or change our game plan for future growth. Taking time to mentally mull over what good came out of the past and how it helped you attain clarity on direction and needs is essential for a good future outcome (harvest).

If you can't see the good result in what initially appeared bad, you will be "toxic" and consumed with stressful thoughts. You will be full of resentment, frustration, irritation and anger, unable to forgive and take responsibility for your situation or observe your present need without judgment or blame. If you are in this state of mind, then you are most likely impatiently rushing into decisions, angry and frustrated, and your life continues to not work out the way you desired. This is not going with the flow of things but rather more like trying to force a square peg into a round hole.

Another way to go wrong is if you sleepwalk through life being passive and unassertive. You are out of touch with your needs and unable to make decisions in excellence. You will be easily led by others and constantly find yourself involved in things you do not wish to be involved in. You will be passive-aggressive and hold anger and resentment inside, blaming others or life for your situation and never grow in excellence.

We label our life experiences and judge them as bad when in fact the opposite, that they are good and could serve us, can be equally true. Being able to fertilize, to see what good can come out of something that was initially perceived as bad, will keep you from suffering. If you rush to plant a new seed or start over without fertilizing (changing your game plan), you will relive the same experience over and over. You are still responsible for the outcome in your life even when you procrastinate or let others make decisions for you.

To help you avoid getting impatient, rushed, angry, frustrated or resentful, as well as to help you get assertive and clear on your direction, consider the following:

1. Be present, calm, clear, honest, and assertive with yourself and others

2. State what you need and why

3. Assert your needs, get clear on your decisions and state your boundaries

4. Stay present, take a deep breath and get clear to make sure a decision you are about to make makes you feel calm, at peace, and assertive rather than stresses you out

5. Think about the consequences of your decisions, words and thoughts

Action/Compete – Summer: Watering and Weeding of the Mind

Once you make a commitment or decision, you need to keep a positive attitude believing in what you are doing. You need to diligently labor for the love of your game. You need to enjoy every moment of practice or competition while striving for excellence. You can separate negative from positive by pulling the weeds before they grow too big, nipping them in the bud. You need to remind yourself the reason you are playing your sport is because it is fun and you love it. If it is not fun, than you need to change your attitude or quit playing.

To help with the weeding, ask yourself and take the following courses of action:

1. Is what I hear true and will it benefit my growth and well-being or not?

2. Is what I intend to speak true, and will it benefit my team's growth and well-being or not?

3. Express your feelings and needs authentically from your heart.

4. Make sure you are calm and authentically enjoying what you are doing, thinking, or feeling.

Focus on (water) what you want – thoughts, beliefs, and actions that make you feel good, happy, and calm, expressing that which is alive in you with passion. Be present and diligently speak and think positive. Always see the glass as half-full. This will bring more good and allow positive emotions to flourish. Question (weed out) stressful thoughts, beliefs, actions, and people. This will bring you joy and peace. Be authentic, real, present, and joyous in your everyday labor of life while focusing on solutions (rather than problems) and expecting that everything always will work out (come to a harvest).

This will require positive focus and present mind. Dwelling on the negative will "water" the weeds and cause them to grow. They can overtake your mind and bring you suffering, poor performance, injury, or disease.

Result – Fall: Mind Realization and Learning

If you planted unfruitful seeds, watered them, and now have merely a garden full of weeds to harvest, it's still not too late to grow in a positive direction by accepting what is (reality), learning from it, letting go and moving on. Are you able to accept your life situation? Are you able to accept what is or what happened? Are you taking responsibility for your life situation without blaming others, being a victim or beating yourself up? If you are disappointed with any outcome, then you are not at peace with the current moment. You are experiencing stress, anxiety, depression or other negative emotions. If this is the case, then you are not realizing what you learned. Your state of mind and your emotions are feedback on whether you are in excellence or not.

Ask yourself:

1. Is my perception of the outcome true? Is it all bad or can I learn something and get stronger from this experience?

2. Did I do the best I could based on my circumstances and what I thought and believed at the time of commitment and action?

3. What did I learn?

Learning from your experiences can turn failure into a harvest. If you do not accept the outcome of your life situation (what is), then you will be filled with disappointment, sadness, grief, resentment, regret, guilt, shame, or embarrassment. You will be stuck in the past and won't be able to move forward. This mental/emotional constipation will cause you much stress, tension, and suffering that, over time, will manifest in an inability to perform, to move on in life, physical injury, and/or disease. The longer you are stuck in this state, the more you suffer. Another way of not accepting a life outcome is when you feel defeated, rejected, apathetic and stop caring. Mental/emotional diarrhea or "not giving a shit" might seem like a good idea at the time, but will cause you to be in denial and move on too fast, hence doom you to experience the same result over and over. This, too, will lead to stress, tension, suffering, poor performance, injury, and eventually disease. In either case, you fail to see the good by not learning the lessons from the outcome (learning = a harvest).

Recovery - Winter: Stillness and Gratitude of the Mind

If you did not reap the "harvest" you expected or desired, you may be fearful of losing what you have: your position on the team, your skill and ability, as well as future opportunities. You may be frozen, paralyzed, unable to take any action, and suffering with tension and pain; fearful of failing again when making another attempt. You can't see the light at the end of the tunnel, the dawn of a new day, or the end of winter.

If you did not harvest, you may also face another imbalance. If you are unable to accept a life outcome and learn from it, if you did not feel you accomplished anything, how can you feel any satisfaction? You may become reckless and impatient, in a rush to start over without any rest. You may try to control things you have no control over. You may fail to appreciate what you have, fail to take care of yourself, your loved ones, or your personal belongings. This controlling, impatient, or unappreciative behavior of not being still will drain your energy and hence cause you to suffer from fatigue, exhaustion, tension, pain, injury, or disease.

1. Remember and apply what you learn; appreciate what you have

2. Have the wisdom to assess what life situations you have control over and which ones you do not

3. Do not drain your energy by dealing with things you have no control over such as the past or the future

4. Mind your own business or things you have control over, and stay out of other people's business, things you have no control over

5. When something comes to an end, rest and be still, cautious, and calm until the next life opportunity (spring) comes around

6. Trust that rest and recovery will help you to get ahead instead of fearing that it will get you behind

Your mind can be your greatest asset

or your worst enemy.

CHAPTER 13

Adrenaline, Friend or Foe?

In the Way of Excellence, all athletic actions, whether it's in practice or competition, are to be **fun** and **played** while **being authentic, passionate and engaged**.

Some athletes are unable to play and have fun when the competition is on. The bigger the stage, the bigger the game, the harder it is for them to play and have fun. Still, almost every athlete has dreamt about playing on the biggest stage like the final drive of a tied Super Bowl or being in the finals at the Olympics. As kids, most of us played out the imaginary event in our own backyard. Once the opportunity turns to reality, many athletes become tense, anxious and scared; while others get so excited they can't wait to shine on the big stage. The difference is the athletes who get anxious and scared do so because they start to **think** about not playing well enough, failing to perform or letting their teammates down. Instead of being present and having fun playing the game, they start to think about the **outcome**; something that has not yet happened. This can be so intense that all fun and creative play is stifled. Having performed to perfection at practice over and over, nothing has changed with their ability. The only thing that has changed is what the athlete is focusing on and their state of mind. Instead of experiencing fun, excitement, and adventure, they perceive danger, worry, disappointment, and fear.

It is normal to feel and experience the rush of **adrenaline** at the time of a big competition. The experience of an adrenaline rush is manifested as butterflies in the stomach, trembling muscles, and heightened awareness. Is the adrenaline friend or foe? Well, it depends on how your mind interprets this initial sensation. Do you get excited and can't wait to play, or do you associate the sensation with something bad? When the experience is that the butterflies and trembling are bad, it can make the athlete feel sick and even immobilize him or her with fear. As an athlete, you need to change your perception and welcome the adrenaline rush with excitement.

The historic Viking warriors who terrorized large parts of Europe around the year 1000 A.D. were fearless in battle. According to their religion, Norse mythology, the Vikings believed that the only way they could enter into Valhalla (the equivalent to our heaven) was to die in battle. In Valhalla, all the fallen warriors entered into an enormous hall to enjoy an eternal feast with the gods. The Vikings were laughing and having fun in battle because there was no fear of dying. Either they won the battle or they died and went to Valhalla. You can imagine the psychological advantage they had in battle laughing and having fun.

When you believe that it's impossible to fail, then you have nothing to lose but missing out on having fun and the opportunity of a lifetime. If you are having a hard time having fun in the big event, then you need to change your inner dialogue and what you believe. Positive affirmations used repetitively can change what you believe as well as how you feel and perform. For example, you can use affirmations like, "I love the excitement and rush of the big game" or "I always win or learn, therefore I always win."

You might play your sport or perform your athletic activity to a lesser degree for the rest of your life. Competing on the highest level is something most athletes experience only for a few years.

What's interesting is that I have heard many athletes testify that once they retired from their main competition what they missed most was the adrenaline rush (butterflies) before the big game. This was all athletes, whether they loved and enjoyed competing on the big stage, or never played well when the pressure was on.

To be in the Way of Excellence, you need to change any destructive belief and behavior, and welcome and love the adrenaline rush when it comes. It means you are alive and about to experience exciting competition on a high level. This is the opportunity you've been dreaming about – take one deep breath and seize the moment.

*When you believe that it's impossible
to fail, then you have nothing to lose
but missing out on having fun and the
opportunity of a lifetime.*

Do Your Job

Knowing how to be and what to do at any moment of any day will keep you on a steady path of excellence; this is doing your job. The fact is that in every moment of every day you are always in one of the four phases; commitment, action, result or recovery and you need to be present in every moment to be in excellence.

Commitment: The beginning of any new action. This could be a new day, workout, game, competition, play, set or repetition. Be clear and commit on how to be (calm and present, clear on your purpose and desire), and what to do (your game plan). Commit to give your best effort and make every day better than the previous one.

Action/Compete: Be authentic and engaged in your every action. Love to compete and challenge yourself to improve. Do what you love or love what you do. Be positive and have fun as you strive for excellence in life and your sport every day.

Result: Learn and grow from every experience and accept the outcome with humility in victory or defeat. If you always do your best and you always learn, then you will always grow and get a lot better with time. True success is the satisfaction that you did your best and you were challenged to grow.

Recovery: Be still and turn off. Be quiet and get deep sleep. Give yourself enough recovery time before you start over. Eat healthy and make sure to get enough protein and nutrients. Make sure to drink enough water to rehydrate. Be grateful for all that you have. Remember and retain what you learned so that you don't have to do your lessons over.

Present Mind: In all phases at all times strive to be calm and present in diaphragmatic breathing, doing one thing at a time in excellence.

Whenever you catch yourself being stressed, tense and not breathing right, you can get immediate relief with just one deep breath. Your job is the present moment. Doing your job is not worrying about the future or regretting the past. Lamenting, regretting and second guessing the past will only make you depressed. The past is an old story that is never good to hold onto. When you worry about the future you are not present in the now. The definition of worrying is praying for what you don't want. Our body moves toward what our mind is occupied on. If you spend more time worrying about the future than being present dealing only with what is in your control and in priority this very moment, then you will never have peace.

Every workout should be better than the previous one. If it's not, then you did not learn your lessons from your previous performance, are not fully recovered (rest and nutrition), lack desire (commitment), or not fully into it (love, passion and fun). Continuing to work out without improving is fruitless and just grooming bad habits.

Being in the Way of Excellence is the same regardless of the outcome of the competition, the score in the game or your placement in the competition. It is the same at all times – COMMIT, COMPETE, LEARN, RECOVER and REMEMBER what you learned.

Then start all over with a new day committing to what worked, changing what did not work. Love every moment to compete and better yourself. Always doing your best based on your circumstances, state of mind and resources, always learning from the outcome regardless if it worked out the way you desired and expected or not.

In the Way of Excellence, life and your athletic activity is truly a journey, not a destination. Peace comes from loving every moment and every step of the way. Every day is a new beginning.

Your job is always to Be present in this moment and Do with excellence what is required in the phase you are in.

Don't get caught up in comparing yourself with others (opponents or teammates). When your head is occupied with what others do or how they perform, then you are no longer present in your business, not doing your job.

In truth, you only compete against yourself, striving to do better and better each and every day. That is the only thing you have control over. If you get a little bit better every day, then you get a lot better over time.

This is the universal law of planting and reaping. As you sow, so shall you reap. There is cause and effect, action and reaction to everything we do. The principle of the seed is to multiply and the farmer keeps growing his harvest and bettering the seeds with every go around. This is the Way of Excellence and the way to be.

Bruce Lee once said, "The greatest help is self-help; there is no other help but self-help – doing one's best, dedicating oneself wholeheartedly to a given task, which happens to have no end but is an ongoing process"

The way to practice kung fu, the Way of Excellence.

True success is the satisfaction that you did your best and you were challenged to grow.

CHAPTER 15

A Day of Excellence

The following is an example of, or recommendation on, how to be in excellence on a daily basis.

Recovery/Winter: Waking Up

When waking up, do not make the mistake of letting your mind immediately rush into everything you have to do that day or instantly reach for your cell phone. Instead, lie in bed (awake, not snoozing), stretch out your body, and use deep breathing to focus on being present. Take a minute to reflect on all the things for which you are grateful. Being in this "attitude of gratitude" helps you realize what is truly important in life before you start your day. This allows for a smooth stress-free transition from rest to action.

Commitment/Spring: Morning

After you eat breakfast, awaken your desires and recommit to master your sport and your life. Take a moment to visualize and get clear on how you want your day to be. Think about what you want out of this day and why. Compose a list of things you need to do, steps on your way. Observe your needs. This can be done in your head or, even better, on paper. Ask yourself if the way you did things yesterday worked or not. If it did, stick to the game plan. If it did not then change your game plan and approach. Do you have any old "crap" (stinking thinking) that is poisoning your attitude? If so, try to see how your "crap" can actually help you grow (**fertilize**). How can you find the silver lining and turn it into something that will make you stronger or better? Things are not done to you; they are done for you to get challenged and grow. Take responsibility for your own life situation and unmet needs rather than judging or blaming others.

Once you have your list, number what you want to get done in order of priority. Commit to a day of excellence, commit to make today better than yesterday. Make sure you stay present (do not let your mind run ahead or go back to the past), stay calm, and be assertive about your direction, desire and needs. Always think of the possible consequences or outcomes of all your actions and spoken words before getting started.

Stay present and calm, never rush into a commitment (**planting a seed**), always breathe deeply and calmly from your belly.

Action/Summer: Day

Stay present, calm, authentic, and fully engaged in your athletic practice or competition. Always be in a state of joy when you play your game or practice your skill. Be excited, love to compete, strive for excellence and mastery every step on your way. Always think positively and expect to get better. Focus on all the parts of your work and training that you enjoy so you can truly labor with love. With every thought, focus (**water**) what you want rather than what you don't want. If your mind is focused on what you don't want then you are watering the weeds. Use discernment to **weed** out negative influences – negative thoughts, negative people, media news, jealousy, and gossip.

Be authentic, look people in the eye and genuinely smile. Be passionate and inspire others around you. Maintain a positive attitude and always see the good in every situation. If you can't say anything good, don't say anything at all. Focus on solutions rather than problems. Focus on breathing deeply from your stomach.

Result/Fall: Evening

As you end your workday and "gather in your crop," ask yourself what you learned today. Things do not always work out the way you intended or expected. If you tend to be hard on yourself, or feel like you never accomplish anything that is good enough, it is good to write down in a journal what you learned and accomplished at the end of each and every day. A **harvest** always will be realized if you focus on what you learned. This will give you a growing sense of self-worth and accomplishment. You do not always get everything on your list done for the day. Some days you might not even get a single thing done. Unless you deliberately attempted to fail and screw things up, you did the best you could under the circumstances you had. Accept the things you cannot change; accept what is. Learn, let go, and keep moving forward. Breathe in, accept what is; breathe out, let go.

Recovery/Winter: Night

Remember that your in-box will never be empty. There always will be something else you can do. The fact is, you will never get done; there is always more to do. Trust that you have all the time you need and that everything will happen when it is supposed to happen (if it is supposed to happen).

Make a point to stop working and thinking about your day and athletic performance at a certain time. Trust that in the long run, **rest** and **recovery** will get you ahead instead of behind. Turn off your cell phone and don't check voice mail, text messages, social media, or e-mail until the next morning when you compose your daily to-do list. Spend quality time with your significant other, children, or pets. Stay present and still with them, and do not allow your mind to drift back to action, future or past. Turn off your TV and read from a book, not a tablet or phone since all electronic devices stimulate rather than relax our nervous system. Use diaphragmatic breathing exercises to become present in resting and to turn off your mind, which may be spinning about the past or the future. Make sure you allow yourself enough hours of quality sleep.

Present Mind/Grounded in the Here and Now: The Present Moment

To be in excellence is to know how to **be** and know what to do in every moment; to be present in **Commitment, Action, Result** and **Recovery** and do only one thing in excellence. Do only what is in your control and priority in that moment. In instances when you have control over nothing, you need to remain present and still until there is something to do that you do have control over. Take a deep breath and enter the Zone with intense awareness of what you are doing in this instance.

The purpose of playing the game is to have fun and strive to master the game. Sometimes life throws you a curve ball. We have to play with the cards we are dealt. Sometimes you lose with "good" cards and other times you may win with "bad" cards, but you always play to have fun and always strive to win.

True success is the satisfaction that comes from doing your best and always learning from the outcome. A day of excellence is to learn something every day. If you always learn then you get a little better every day and over time you get a lot better. The truth is that you never reach mastery; you could always get better. Life is not about mastery or winning, it is about striving for mastery, thriving at being challenged, competing and enjoying the journey.

Every day is a new beginning, a new day to start fresh and commit to be in excellence. When you are present doing the right thing at the right time, then you are in the Way of Excellence. It will help you get a little better every day and a lot better with time. The Way of Excellence will teach you that it is not about the outcome but the excellence in the step you take right here right now, the Zone. This is the only thing you ever truly have control over.

Life is not a destination; it's a journey.

Every Day is a New Beginning in a Never Ending Strive for Excellence

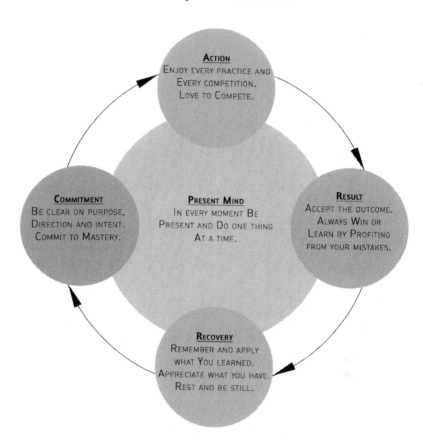

ACTION
ENJOY EVERY PRACTICE AND
EVERY COMPETITION.
LOVE TO COMPETE.

COMMITMENT
BE CLEAR ON PURPOSE,
DIRECTION AND INTENT.
COMMIT TO MASTERY.

PRESENT MIND
IN EVERY MOMENT BE
PRESENT AND DO ONE THING
AT A TIME.

RESULT
ACCEPT THE OUTCOME.
ALWAYS WIN OR
LEARN BY PROFITING
FROM YOUR MISTAKES.

RECOVERY
REMEMBER AND APPLY
WHAT YOU LEARNED.
APPRECIATE WHAT YOU HAVE.
REST AND BE STILL.

In accordance with the ancient teachings, the Way of Excellence is about committing to mastery of a cause and realizing it is a never-ending project.

CHAPTER 16

Closing Story

In closing, I'd like to share a story. There once lived a very wise, old Shaolin monk in a small village high up in the Tibetan Mountains. He was providing wisdom and protection for the villagers and the villagers believed there wasn't a secret of life he didn't know. So one day, some of the rebellious teenagers in the village planned a cruel and evil trick on the old man – they wanted to catch the old monk being wrong and shame him publicly.

Their plan was to catch a bird and hold it behind their backs while asking the old master if the bird they held in their hands was alive or dead. If he said dead, they would let it fly away. If he said it was alive, they would break its neck behind their backs and hold it up dead in front of the old man's eyes.

After catching a bird, the youngsters approached the old monk, and with a nervous stutter they said, "Oh, wise and mighty one, please tell us, is this bird we hold behind our backs alive or dead?"

The wise old monk took his time to answer, his eyes piercing the eyes of the nervous teenagers. Then he answered, "The matter is all in your hands."

And so the knowledge of how to use this ancient wisdom of this book to find your Zone, reach your potential and perform in excellence is now in your hands.

This wisdom could set you free to perform and have fun. You could diligently practice these simple lessons on a daily basis to experience continued joy and growth in your athletic pursuit, or you could forget what you read and let this knowledge die.

Above all, do not take yourself too serious and have fun playing the game.

About the Author

Tobe Hanson

Sports Injury Specialist and Performance Coach

When I was a kid growing up in Stockholm, Sweden, I dreamed of being a professional hockey or soccer player. At 14, I had the crushing realization that my childhood dream was not to be. My dad inspired me to start weight training so I'd have another athletic activity to enjoy. Weight training helped me build both confidence and muscles, but it also inspired me to further investigate the function, potential, and performance of the human body and mind.

At 21, I was pondering what to do for a living. With my love of athletics and my curiosity about the potential of the human body, I was searching for a profession in this field. I considered becoming a physical therapist, chiropractor or PE teacher, when out of curiosity I attended a lecture about ancient Chinese medicine and applied kinesiology. The experience from this lecture made me realize that healing pain and enhancing human performance through a holistic approach, was the path for me. I felt there were many hidden pearls of wisdom in this ancient Chinese medicine that were seemingly forgotten or misinterpreted.

I have spent three-and-a-half decades practicing and studying acupressure, trigger point therapy, ancient Eastern medicine, sports medicine, anatomy, physiology, kinesiology, psychology, theology, applied kinesiology, reflexology, and body work. My fascination with muscles and knowledge about kinesiology, as well as ancient Chinese medicine, led me on an extensive search for a better therapy. This search led to the development of my own **Hands-On** therapy.

Hanson Muscle Therapy – HMT (www.TobeHanson.com), a new and holistic approach to sports medicine, is a feedback-based manual therapy for immediate pain relief, injury rehabilitation, and performance enhancement. Since 1983, I have had close to 120,000 patient visits and currently have a four-week waiting list for an appointment. I've grown my practice prior to the internet and search engines simply by word of mouth without advertising, yellow page ads, or even a phone directory listing. Orthopedic surgeons, family doctors, chiropractors, dentists, athletic trainers, personal trainers, acupuncturists, and massage therapists refer patients to me on a daily basis and my services are frequently sought after by professional athletes from NHL, NFL, MLB, PGA, triathlons, mixed martial arts, college, and recreational athletes. I have been part of the San Jose Sharks NHL medical staff for more than 10 years and currently work weekly with the Stanford University football team.

In HMT, muscles are used as feedback to detect tension in the body and mind. Tension leads to pain and injury of the body and decreased or destructive performance of the body and mind. The muscles of our body enable us to move and they also act as an armor that protects us. It is in this armor we find the dents from use, overuse, and abuse.

Whenever our body or mind is experiencing stress or tension it will manifest as hypersensitive cracks in the-armor – knots in our muscles. These knots are called trigger or acupressure points and act as circuit breakers that tense up when overloaded. No one has pain, anxiety, or depression for no reason; in the same way, no one experiences failure, sub-par performance or unhappiness for no reason. There is cause and effect, action and reaction, meaning and purpose with everything that happens in life. In my practice of HMT, I learned how to localize points of tension, interpret the cause of the tension, and release the tension for immediate pain relief and improved performance. Teaching my patients the cause of their pain and failure helped them realize what they needed to do to change their way; behavior, beliefs, and attitude.

In my search for a better way to heal pain and improve performance, I discovered a way to explain forgotten secrets passed down from ancient Chinese Acupuncture masters. It took me 30 years of research, over 100,000 patient visits, and six years of writing, to clarify 5000–year-old Chinese wisdom in modern Western terms. In my book, *The Four Seasons Way of Life, Ancient Wisdom for Healing and Personal Growth* (www.TobeHanson.com) those forgotten secrets are explained in an easy to understand metaphor. It is about timing and doing the right thing, at the right time, in harmony with our surroundings and circumstances. Our patterns of behavior explain the outcome of our lives.

The writings in this book, *Athletes Way of Excellence*, are about how to use Ancient Chinese Wisdom to achieve athletic peak performance and how to be in the Zone. The sources of the information in this book are the same ancient Chinese wisdom and principles as in my first book. After 33 years of working in holistic sports medicine, I have studied thousands of athletes and witnessed first-hand the cause and effect of their behavior and beliefs in victory or defeat. *Athlete's Way of Excellence* **teaches 12 lessons** of timing; how to be, as well as what to do and when to do it.

This book is dedicated to my love for sports and athletics and it is my hope that it shall provide the wisdom to young and aspiring athletes that most athletes never fully learn or learn too late in their career.

Today, I have been building my body for over 40 years and have never gone more than two weeks without a workout. Natural bodybuilding and pure living has made me fit and strong in body and mind. It has given me peace and stability in times of turmoil and it has become a labor of love for a lifetime.

The mind-muscle connection in training has become like meditation or like the 2000-year-old ancient Japanese Zen art of caring for a bonsai tree.

The beauty is that you are never finished; the training truly becomes a journey rather than a destination. Like Arnold Schwarzenegger said in the movie Pumping Iron, "Bodybuilding is like being a sculptor sculpting your own body." Add a little here, remove a little there, all while enjoying the exercise of body and peace of mind. Being fit in body and mind are necessary to be in the Way of Excellence. Any athletic body type is a beautiful and amazing creation.

There is a common prejudice toward bodybuilders, and sometimes athletes in general, that they are unintelligent, narcissistic meatheads. On my path, and through my search and studies, I found that the body is just a shell or a vehicle that allows us to move around in this world. Everyone's body will eventually break down and decompose. It's not good to associate who we are based on our body or athletic ability since this will cause great depression, as age eventually catches up with us. Who we truly are is something whole and beautiful that is not subject to time. This, of course, does not mean that we shall abuse and ruin the body we have. Appreciating the fitness you have and taking great care of your body will improve your quality of life, improve your performance, strengthen your immune system, and slow down your aging, all being the Way of Excellence. There is an athletic body in all of us.

I remember a student in one of my classes asking me if I saw the German museum exhibit; "Body Worlds" (a traveling exposition of preserved real human bodies that has been skinned to show the muscles; the bodies have been preserved through plastination). I replied, "Yes, I did. Wasn't it remarkable?" He said. "What was amazing to me was that every one of the exhibiting bodies had a six pack!" I replied, "Every human being has a six pack, it's just that in most people it is covered by fat and can't be seen." Firm, toned muscles with low body fat reflects a balanced metabolism, diet, and exercise routine as well as a balanced mind and emotions. In other words, there is a toned muscular athletic body in all of us. It is never too late to start taking care of the body you have. If you're already a fit athlete as you are reading this, remember never to take your body, fitness or genetics for granted. You too can stay fit for life and perform at a high level for years to come.

Today at 58, when I look back at the road I traveled, I marvel at how everything happened for a reason. I might never have been the great athlete I aspired to be, but now I am helping world-class athletes perform better. To aid fellow human beings in their healing and to inspire growth on both a physical, mental, emotional and spiritual plane is more fulfilling than anything I could ever have dreamt of doing for a living. In fact, I would not want to be any other person throughout history than me right here or do anything else than what I am doing right now.

With the writing of this book and the opening of my new HMT Clinic, I hope to revolutionize the fields of sports medicine, sports performance, and sports psychology.

Photo Credit: © Ralph DeHaan • From left to right: Tobe Hanson, Mark Hastings, Krystal Ricci, Alceu Vieira, Anthony Edwards

Tobe Hanson (far left) at 56 competing at the 2016 San Jose bodybuilding championship for the first time after 40 years of natural bodybuilding training. Living in the Way of Excellence.

Photo Courtesy of USAMuscleWomen.com

Tobe's wife, best friend, assistant editor of this book, personal trainer, natural bodybuilder and physique competitor, Sue Epperson, competing at the 2013 Nationals at 55. www.MuscleMakerSue.com

Suggested Reading

- Huang Ti Nei Ching Su Wen: The Yellow Emperor's Classic of Internal Medicine by Ilza Veith
- Tao Te Ching by Lao Tzu
- The Four Seasons Way of Life - Ancient Wisdom for Healing and Personal Growth by Tobe Hanson
- Traditional Acupuncture: The Law of the Five Elements by Dr. Dianne M. Connelly
- The Warrior Within: The Philosophies of Bruce Lee by John Little
- Wooden: A Lifetime of Observations and Reflections On and Off the Court by Coach John Wooden with Steve Jamison
- Integrative Medicine by Dr. David Rakel
- Way of the Peaceful Warrior by Dan Millman
- The Power of Now by Eckhart Tolle

Are You ready to commit to the Way

of Excellence in Your life?

Spreading the Word

Dear Reader,

Thank you for reading this book.

For more than three decades, I have worked on the Four Seasons metaphor with a burning desire to heal body and mind, improve human peace (being), and performance (doing) to enhance personal growth, improve quality of life and live life in excellence.

Athlete's Way of Excellence can be applied for excellence of all things in life. It can be applied to achieve excellence as a husband, wife, parent, and friend, as well as excellence in your profession, your career, your health and your fitness.

If this book has been helpful to you, please share it with everyone you believe could profit from it. I would be grateful if you tweet, write reviews on Amazon.com and other book retailer distributors and blogs of how the information in this book helped you and how it may help others as well.

To inquire about bulk discounts for your clients, students, and/or teammates or to invite me to speak at your event, please contact us at www.TobeHanson.com.

Follow me on Twitter @TobeHanson.

Thank you for your support in spreading the word.

My sincere gratitude,
Tobe Hanson

Also by Tobe Hanson

The Four Seasons Way of Life

Ancient Wisdom for Healing and Personal Growth

Tobe Hanson

Follow Tobe on Twitter
@TobeHanson